Bhavishya Purana earns a special distinction by being the only *Purana* that is based on the 'predictions'. It mostly tells us what 'will be' from the time it was compiled in. Hence oracles and prophecies abound in this *Purana*. Even though other *Puranas* also delve occasionally in future-telling, they all seem to have borrowed the futuristic section from this Purana only. The present edition of *Bhavishya Purana* is the abridged or condensed version of the three *Puranas* known as 'Bhavishya Purana', 'Bhavishyati Purana' and 'Bhavishyottara Purana'. It is also believed to have been the only *Purana* that has continued to evolve for more than 2000 years.

DIAMOND POCKET BOOKS PRESENTS
RELIGION AND SPIRITUALITY BOOKS

G.D. Bhudhiraja
Does God Exists? 95.00
Dr. B.D. Sharma
Rudraksh Therapy 95.00
Dinesh Chandra
Hinduism (The Dawn of Civilization) 150.00
Dr. Bhojraj Dwivedi
Diamond Annual Horoscope 2009 .... 125.00
Surojit Mahanabolis
Himalayan Pilgrimage 395.00
Pavan Choudhary & Charushilla Narula
Kabir, Reincarnated Success Sutras
for the 21st Century 150.00
Subramanian Swamy
Ramsetu: Symbol of National Unity 195.00
Hindus Under Siege: The way Out 150.00
S. N. Mathur
Gautam Buddha (The Spiritual Light of Asia)
[4 Colours - 20x30x8] 295.00
The Diamond Book of Hindu Gods & Goddesses
(4 Colur-20×30×8) 295.00
Hindu Fast and Festival (4 Colur-20×30×8) 395.00
Ek Onkar Satnam (4 Colur-20×30×8) 395.00
Ed. Acharya Bhagwan Dev
Sanskar Vidhi 125.00
B.K. Chaturvedi
Gods & Goddesses of India 150.00
Shiv Purana 95.00
Vishnu Purana 95.00
Markandeya Purana 75.00
Bhavishya Purana 75.00
Narad Purana 75.00
Shrimad Bhagvat Purana 95.00
Devi Bhagvat Purana 75.00
Garud Purana 75.00
Agni Purana 75.00
Kalki Purana 75.00
Ling Purana 75.00
Varah Purana 75.00
Vayu Puran 75.00
Brahamvevart Purana 75.00
Padam Purana 75.00
Koorma Purana 95.00
Skand Purana 95.00
Matsya Purana 95.00
Harivansh Purana 95.00
S. K. Sharma
The Brilliance of Hinduism 125.00
Sanskar Vidhi (Arya Samaj) 125.00
Dr. Rajbali Pandey
Rigveda 95.00
Samveda 95.00
Yajurveda 95.00
Atharvveda 95.00
Dr. B.R. Kishore
Essence of Vedas 195.00
Hinduism 125.00
Mahabharata 75.00
Ramayana 75.00
Supreme Mother Goddess Durga (4 Color) .. 95.00
Acharya Vinay Singhal
Kali Poojan 95.00
Chandi Path 95.00
Manish Verma
Fast & Festivals of India 95.00
S. P. Bansal
Gajanan 75.00
Lord Rama 75.00

Prof. Gurpret Singh
Soul of Sikhism 125.00
Shiv Sharma
Philosophy of Islam 125.00
Soul of Jainism 125.00
F.S. Growse
Mathura & Vrindavan, The Mystical Land
of Lord Krishna (8 Colour photos) 495.00
Udit Sharma
Teachings & Philosophy of Buddha 150.00
Manan Sharma
Buddhism (Teachings of Buddha) 150.00
Universality of Buddha 150.00
Anurag Sharma
Life Profile & Biography of Buddha 150.00
Thus Spake Buddha 150.00
S.P. Ojha
Sri-Ram-Charit Manas 95.00
Chakor Ajgaonkar
Realm of Sadhana (What Saints & Masters Say) 30.00
K.H. Nagrani
A Child from the Spirit World Speaks 10.00
Dr. Giriraj Shah
Gurus, Philosopher, Mystics &
Saints of India - I & II 195.00
Glory of Indian Culture 195.00
R.P. Hingorani
Chalisa Sangreh (Roman) 60.00
Acharya Vipul Rao
Srimad Bhagwat Geeta (Sanskrit & English) 75.00
Dr. Bhavansingh Rana
108 Upanishad (In press) 150.00
Eva Bell Barer
Quiet Talks with the Master 60.00
Joseph J. Ghosh
Adventures with Evil Spirits 80.00
Dr. S.P. Ruhela
Fragrant Spiritual Memories of a Karma Yogi .. 100.00
Sri Shridi Sai Baba: The Universal Master 95.00
Yogi M.K. Spencer
Rishi Ram Ram 100.00
Oneness with God 90.00
H. Seereeram
Fundamentals of Hinduism 250.00
Dr. Gopal Sharma
Ways to Attract Wealth 95.00
Jilliana Raymond
God's Toolbox 95.00
Dr. Satyajit
The Holy Book of Hindu Religion 50.00
Mahesh Sharma
Tales from Vedas 95.00
Tales from Purana 95.00
Tales from Upnishad 95.00
V.K. Chaturvedi
Tales from Ramayana - Mahabharata 95.00
Narendra Kumar Sinha
The Story of Rama 250.00
Sri Krit Bhai
Navratan Bodh Katha 95.00
Rekha Sigi
Sri Krishna: The Ascetic (Biography) 95.00
P.B. Paliwal
Message of Vedas 150.00
Message of Purana 150.00
Message of Upnishad 150.00
Message of Darshan 150.00

DIAMOND BOOKS X-30, Okhla Industrial Area, Phase-II, New Delhi-110020,
Phone : 011-40712100, Fax : 011-41611866, E-mail : sales@dpb.in, Website : www.dpb.in

Bhavishya Purana

B.K. Chaturvedi

DIAMOND BOOKS

No part of this book may be reproduced or transmitted in any form or by any means electronic or mechanical including photocopying or recording or by any information storage and retrieval systems without prior permission in writing from Diamond Pocket Books (P) Ltd.

ISBN : 81-288-0598-3

© Publisher

Published by	: Diamond Pocket Books (P) Ltd.
	X-30, Okhla Industrial Area, Phase-II
	New Delhi-110020
Phone	: 011-41611861-65, 40712100
Fax	: 011-41611866
E-mail	: sales@dpb.in
Website	: www.dpb.in
Edition	: 2010
Printed by	: Adarsh Printers, Shahdara, Delhi-110032

Bhavishya Purana

by : B.K. Chaturvedi

Contents

Preface 7

Introduction 9

1. Creation And Ceremonies 11
2. Stories Highlighting The Efficacy Of The Vratas 23
3. Education, Marriage And Temples 45
4. The Past Present And Future Dynasties 56
5. The Satyanarain Katha And Other Tales 72
6. Epilogue 80

Glossary 83

Preface

The Puranas are not only the tomes of mythological stories and ancient records but they also reveal the progress of the thought process of the Indian social milieu.

They contain literature, grammar, science and almost every branch of knowledge that developed in this part of the world. They are eighteen in number and believed to have been compiled by the renowned Sage Vedavyas. In fact barring the Ramayana which is the creation of the renowned Sage Valmiki, almost all the sacred Hindu scriptures had issued from his (Vedavyas's) pen only. After having composed the Mahabharata, Vedavyas was not content with the stories that he had recounted. He felt as though the stories recounted needed a wider explanation. Then be composed the eighteen Mahapuranas. These texts have among them as many as more than four lakh shlokas. Of course there have been quite many an interpolation, but all the Puranas' authorship is basically attributed to him only. Obviously so much of writing is beyond the apparent capacity of one individual. This fact led the scholars believe that Vedavyas was merely a title, conferred on the most learned and unbiased person of every era. The last Vedavyas was Krishna Dwaipayana, the son of an illegitimate union between sage Parashar and Satyavati, the daughter of the headman of the boat-rowers who lived along the banks of the river Yamuna.

The Bhavishya Purana, the ninth in the list of the Mahapurana, is a short Purana, containing about fourteen thousand couplets.

For a Purana to be a Mahapurana, it must contain five characteristics (Pancha Lakshana). That is, the text must describe five different subjects: original creation of the universe ('sarga'), the periodical process of destruction and re-creation ('pratisarga'), the various eras of Manu (Manvantaras), the genealogical details of the two prominent dynasties: the solar and the lunar dynasties (Surya and Chandra Vansha respectively) and the ritualistic details of the noble deeds to be performed in every era. Although the Bhavishya Purana does not quite adhere to this rule of 'Pancha Lakshanas', it is treated as a Mahapurana. It is because, going by this definition, none of the Puranas, save the Vishnu Purana, fully conform to this norm. The Bhavishya Purana comes under the category of a Rajasika Purana.

The Bhavishya Purana earns a special distinction by being the only Purana that is based on the 'predictions'. It mostly tells us what 'will be' from the time it was compiled in. Hence oracles and prophecies abound in this Purana. Even though other Puranas also delve occasionally in future-telling, they all seem to have borrowed the futuristic section from this Purana only. It is believed that the present edition of the Bhavishya Purana is the abridged or condensed version of the three Puranas known as 'Bhavishya Purana', 'Bhavishyati Purana' and 'Bhavishyottara Purana'.

It is also believed to have been the only Purana that has continued to evolve for more than 2000 years. In fact the allusion incorporated in this Purana as prophecies—predicting not only the happenings of the Medieval Ages but even referring about the British Raj in India—make its authenticity suspect as an ancient tome of the sacred knowledge. The scholars, however, generally opine that its basic text has grown over a period of two millennia. Perhaps after its editing during the Gupta Reign (3rd-4th AD) it continued to suffer interpolations or additions till as late as 1850 AD.

Whatever be the date of its final compilation it presents an interesting study. It shows how the interpolations had Sanskritised the Prakrata or even Persian-Arabic term (viz Ahlaad for the chivalrous hero of the Middle Ages called Alha (of Alha-Vdal fame) and Timirling for Taimurlung] to make the interpolation acquire a sheen of authenticity.

The chapterisation of the present work doesn't follow the original text order but it clubs all the details of a single activity (like Vrata or Daan) under one heading. It is hoped that our discerning readership would find this arrangement rather easily comprehensible and logical and accord this work a warm welcome.

Introduction

The 'Bhavishya Purana' is perhaps the most controversial Purana from the point of view of its authenticity. It has a variety of versions available with at least three names: Bhavishya Purana, Bhavishyati Purana and Bhavishyottara Purana. Moreover it is the only Purana which touches ('forecasts') events as late as that occurring in the end of the 19th century AD. Also, since its text had undergone a variety of interpolations, the haphazard references of various events, rituals and stories that spread all over the text, it has been a monumental task to make its contents easily comprehensible for the modern curious reader.

Nevertheless, with all these difficulties, an endeavour has been made to make the reader get the gist of its contents in a logical way. That is why this work is littered with copious foot-notes because it was felt that unless the foot-notes or explanations within the parenthesis are not given the whole text may appear pointless and to some extent quite boring. The equivalent prevalent names of the Sanskritised names of the main characters of the stories have also been explained in order to help the reader derive the right reference to the allusion. At times, due to paucity of space, the stories that are repeated in other Puranas without any change in the sequence have been briefly referred to with a passing reference to their availability in other Puranas. Some of the stories or details which appeared to be lacking sense and relevance have been only briefly referred to. The desirous readers may consult the original to get the full details.

All said and done, it has been quite an onerous task to give the essence of the Bhavishya Purana in this slender volume. But the author is, indeed, grateful to Shri Narendra Kumar Ji of Diamond Pocket Books who allowed him total freedom. It is hoped that the discerning readers would add this work to their personal library—like they have accorded the warm welcome to the other Puranas of the same series. No matter how but these Puranas do provide us a peep into our past that eventually went to form the norms of our modern society. For, as Santyana opined in his famous 'Life of Reason', "those who cannot remember the past are condemned to repeat it."

—B.K. Chaturvedi

Creation and Ceremonies

Maharshi Vedavyas, the son of Sage Parashar and maiden Satyavati, had created or compiled many Puranas. Although they all are quite merit bestowing, yet when the group of the leading sages including sages Bhrigu, Vashishtha, Pulastya, Pulaha, Kratu, Parashar, etc. reached near king Shatanika, a disciple of Vyas only, they asked the king to recite to them some such sacred text as could ensure final release to the listener's soul.

"It is indeed true that I am a disciple of sage Vedavyas and have learnt much from my guru," replied Shatanika. "But that which you wish to learn about still cludes me. Let me ask the great sage as to which is that sacred knowledge whose recital may fulfil your heart's desire."

When Shatanika asked Vedavyas about it, he said: "I have already taught all this to my disciple, Sumantu. Why don't you seek Sumantu's guidance for this? May be he tells you all that you wish to learn."

When Shatanika went to Sumantu, a long dialogue began between the two which forms the basic body of this sacred text called 'Bhavishya Purana'. Sumantu enlightened all the sages, saying that this is the Purana "whose recital or learning redeems a man from all his sins and he gets the merit that accrues to the one who performs an Ashwamedha Yagya. Only the Brahmins and the Kshatriyas can study it while the Shoodras can only listen to it."

Then Sumantu, revealing about this great 'Bhavishya Purana', said: "The lakshana (identifying symptoms) of a Purana are five sections or Parva. First is Brahma Parva, second Vaishnava, third Shaiva, fourth Twashtha and the fifth Pratisarga. These sections contain not only the details about creation and destruction but genealogical charts of the famous dynasties, the commentaries of the four Vedas, six parts of the Veda-knowledge (Vedanga), Meemansa, jurisprudence, fourteen disciplines of knowledge which, if included with Ayurveda, Dhanurveda, Gandharva Shastra and Artha Shashtra become eighteen in number. Then he started the narration with details about the Creator.

[These Puranas are generally divided into three categories: Sattvika, Rajas and Tamas[1]. That Purana which extols the virtues of Lord Vishnu is held to be Sattvika, of Brahma Rajasika and of Shiv Tamasika. Since Bhavishya Purana extols the virtues of Brahma it is said to be the Rajasika Purana.]

There is no god like Brahma, no teacher like him. The sacred Vedas are his conceptions. He is the god of wisdom. His consort is Sarasvati who is held to be the goddess of wisdom.

The learned should devote themselves to Brahma. Those, and only those, versed in the Vedas should instal his images and build temples dedicated to him. A person who constructs a temple to Brahma goes straight to heaven and enjoys divine pleasures. If a person sweeps one of Brahma's temples, he attains the objects of his desire. Even if one sweeps the temple dedicated to Brahma with evil intention, he also goes to heaven.

Prior to the creation of the universe, there was darkness and water everywhere. In this primordial darkness, Brahma created himself through his own energy. Since he was born (bhoo) from himself (Swayam), Brahma's one epithet is also Swayambhoo.

It was Brahma who created all the beings that populate the universe. From his psychic (mental) powers he created the great sages like Maarichi, Atri, Angira, Pulastya, Pulaha, Kratu, Vashishtha, Bhrigu, Daksha and Narada. [This Bhavishya Purana differs from other mythological accounts in the sense that while other Puranas often mention that Brahma was born from a lotus that sprouted out of Vishnu's navel, it calls him Swayambhoo. In other accounts, Brahma's birth is also attributed to a universal egg (anda); none of these accounts is mentioned in this Purana.]

Brahma created Ganesh (It is again different from what other Puranas claim).

In ancient times, success automatically crowned human efforts. There was no need of any divine favour. People

---

1. Read details ahead.

could do what they wanted to do without encountering any difficulties. Even if there arose any they could be easily met with and overcome.

People, on account of getting success rather easily, developed an overblown sense of self-importance. They became proud, overconfident and irreverent.

Brahma got worried seeing his creations developing this sense of overbearing manners. "I must do something about this," thought Brahma. "I must check their arrogance. I will have to create a deity without worshipping whom the humans would not get success." It was then he created Ganesh, the lord of all obstructions. With his creation, no longer ordinary men and women were able to resolve their difficulties on their own. They now needed help and blessings from Lord Ganesh. It became customary to worship Ganesh to ensure success is any endeavour. He became the first god to be invoked at the undertaking of any venture. Hence Ganesh came to be called 'Lord of all obstructions' or Vighneshwar as also the 'bestower of success' (Siddhadata).

Ganesh gives extraordinary powers to those who are his devotees. To please Ganesh, one has to purify oneself through baths and offer the god food and flowers. Donation in alms to the Brahmins also became a necessary act to propitiate this god.

However, Ganesh is displeased if a person dreams of bathing in oil or is sad without reason. He is also displeased when rulers do not rule, teachers do not teach or students do not study. Also, agriculture and trade do not prosper when Ganesh is not worshipped before hand.

[Curiously enough, this Purana is unique in that it attributes Ganesh's creation to Brahma and not to Shiv or Parvati]

Surya and Sangya's Story

According to Bhavishya Purana the most important god is the sun god or Surya.

Telling about this god's creation, Sumantu told Shatanika the following details:

To ensure that creation could sustain itself Brahma divided his body into two parts. The male half came to be known as Swayambhoo Manu and the female as Shataroopa. Through his mental or psychic powers, Manu gave birth to ten sons. Since these sons became the lords ('pati') over all the subjects that were there in the universe (praja) they came to be known as Prajapatis. One of theme was Daksha.

Aditi was one of the daughters of Daksha. Sage Kashyapa was Brahma's son and Aditi was married to Kashyapa. This union eventually produced an egg, which for many days remained almost dead or inactive. Kashyapa and Aditi thought that egg to be a worthless, dead object. Kashyapa minutely observed that egg and declared: "The egg (anda) is not dead (mrita)". Eventually when the sun-god emerged from the egg, he earned the epithet Martanda, (an acronym coined from the words 'mrita' 'anda'). Then the sun god began to develop gloriously. When he came of age, Kashyapa thought of his marriage.

The divine architect, Vishwakarma, had a daughter named Sangya (also called Sanjna by Sanskrit spelling). She was married to Surya (the sun god). Their children were Yama, Yamuna and Manu [This Manu was Savarni Manu and not to be confused with Swayambhoo Manu].

Although Sangya had begotten three sons, she always felt difficulty in Surya's company due to his dazzling energy. Unable to withstand this brilliance, she thought of a trick. She created her exact replica of darker complexion, a woman called Chhaya (shadow) (also called Nikshubha), out of her own body. There was no little difference between the two; if beheld casually, it was impossible to tell the two apart.

Then Sangya told Chhaya: "It is impossible for me to bear my husband's brilliance. Please stay here at my place and impersonate myself. Take care of my children, and under no circumstances should you reveal the truth to my husband."

"I will do as you wish, lady," said Chhaya, adding, "I shall not reveal the truth until I get cursed. But the moment I am subjected to any curse by your husband or anybody else, I shall reveal the truth that I am not Sangya but her exact replica, Chhaya."

Sangya knew that her secret was not likely to be exposed. So she accepted the condition and left. For a while she stayed with her father Vishwakarma without telling him that she had deserted her husband, Surya. Initially Vishwakarma thought as though his daughter had come to pay him a visit. But when days went by and Sangya showed no intention of returning to her husband's place. Vishwakarma's suspicions were aroused. In order to allay these suspicions, she left her father's house. In order to escape identification of her by anybody, she adopted the form of a mare and began to dwell in the region called Uttarakuru [The Bhavishya Purana again differs from the standard text given in the Matsya Purana which says that after becoming a mare Sangya stayed in a Maru Pradesh (desert)].

Chhaya also bore two children for Surya whose names were Shrutukarma (known as Shani or Saturn) and Tapti.

[In some versions of Bhavishya Purana it is claimed that Savarni Manu was also the product of the union of Surya and Chhaya. It gives an explanation that the name Savarni was derived from the meaning 'Sa' + 'Varni' which means of the same complexion which is hardly tenable].

One day Chhaya grew angry with Yama, the son of the union of Sangya and Surya, and cursed him. This made Suryadeva rather suspicious as no real mother could curse her own son. Moreover, one day Tapti and Yamuna also had a quarrel on some point.

Enraged Tapti said: "I curse you that you will become a river."

"So you shall also be", thundered Yamuna.

[This episode, in the Markandeya Purana, has been described in a different manner[1].]

Consequently Tapti became a river. Sangya was angry seeing her daughter suffering the curse pronounced by the daughter of her co-wife. So in order to protect her children she also gave vent to her anger on the innocent Yama, the real brother of Yamuna. Yama was already wroth with his

---

1. These differences in reporting various episodes in different manners in the Puranas prove that they were compiled by different groups of persons in different periods. Although it is claimed that during the Gupta Age all the Puranas were edited, this does not appear to be a truth.

step-mother owing to her foul attitude towards his real brother and sister. When rebuked by his step-mother, he couldn't check her temper and raised his foot to kick his step-mother.

At this Chhaya cursed Yama: "As soon as you put that foot down, insects will devour it. It will wither."

At that point Surya reached there. He already had suspicions about Chhaya (whom he thought to be Sangya) acting as real mother to his elderly progeny. What egged on it was the complaint of Yama: "Sire, she has always been unfair to me. I admit that my raising up my foot to hit her is surely an unpardonable offence. But have you ever seen any true mother cursing her own children? And please do something to negate her curse to my foot."

Expressing his inability to entirely negate the curse, Surya said: "But I assure you that even if insects suck blood from your foot and devour the flesh your feet shall remain as sturdy as ever. They will not wither. As for my daughters Tapti and Yamuna, who have to become rivers, I bless them that they will be as sacred as to wash away the sin of the bathers and Yamuna will be as holy as the Ganga would be and Tapti as Narmada."

Thereafter Surya admonished Chhaya: "How can a mother discriminate among her children?" He was about to curse Chhaya and so Chhaya's condition of keeping the secret of Sangya's absence was violated. So she told Surya that she was not Sangya but Chhaya as his previous wife had deserted him.

Surya was shocked. The immediately left in the quest of Sangya. Surya went to his father-in-law, Vishwakarma, to look for Sangya. Through his mental powers Vishwakarma could know as to what had happened. He told Surya that Sangya had left him because she couldn't bear his radiance. "Let me cut a part of your radiance so that you could become bearable for my daughter." Surya agreed to have this done. The excess energy was sliced off by Vishwakarma. This entire exercise was undertaken in the land of Shakadwipa. But Surya's sliced-off energy was not wasted. From it were cast the Chakra Sudarshana which was gifted to Vishnu and a trident which was eventually given to Lord Shiv.

A little short of his radiance in order to eliminate the cause of inconvenience to his first wife, Sangya, and having learnt about her being available in the region called Uttarakuru in the form of a mare, Surya adopted the form of a horse and met her. In that form they produced a pair of male issues who were named Ashwinikumaras (litterally, the sons of a horse pair). They were extremely handsome and became the physicians of the gods. [The Mahabharat says that the younger Pandavas, viz., Nakula and Sahdeva, sons of Pandu's younger wife, Madri, were the incarnations of these two divine physicians.]

Following Surya and Sangya's returning their normal forms they produced another son named Raivanta. He was born, according to this Purana, astride a horse and donning an armour with arms in his hand.

This section of the Bhavishya Purana extols Surya as much as to relegate even the super Trinity, Brahma, Vishnu and Mahesh to even a lower position. It says that Brahma himself told sage Yagyavalkya, "Surya is the god who dispels the darkness of the whole world and is the source of light for all the three realms. Eternal and omniscient he is the founder, preserver and destroyer of the universe. He is the God of the gods—the supreme one, he whom no god can dare match. He grants salvation to those who worship him with full faith and adulation".

The Process of Creation

In the Primordial stage Lord Narayana divided his body in two parts: one male and the other female. These two male and female parts together created the whole universe. The beings of the universe are of four varieties: Jarayuj (placental), Andaj (born out of an egg), Swedaja (sweat-born) and Udibhaj (sprouting from beneath the ground). These are the four means of birth for the entire creation. Those born in a psychic or through mental powers (like Narada etc. whom Brahma created through his psychic powers) are a different means of creation.

Telling them details Sumantu told Raja Shatanika that in the beginning of the Kalpa, Lord Supreme creates the world which is destroyed at its end. One Kalpa is equal to Lord's one day. Then telling about the unit of time the sage said: "18 Nimesha are equal to one 'Kashtha'. Thirty such 'Kashtha' measure one 'Kala'. Thirty 'Kalas' make one 'Kshana' (moment). Twelve Kshanas make one Muhurta. Thirty Muhurta measure one 'Aho-ratri' (day-night). Three seasons measure one 'Ayana' and two 'Ayanas' measure one year. The day time for all beings is meant for activity and the night time for sleeping or dreaming. Each month is made up of two fortnights. The bright fortnight is called 'Shukla-Paksha' and the dark fortnight 'Krishna-Paksha'. The 'Ayana' when the sun tilts northwards is called 'Uttarayana' and when southwards, it is called 'Dakshinayana'. One mortal Yuga is equal to Brahma's one 'Day-night'. A Satya Yuga contains 4000 Brahma's years, Treta 3000 years, Dwapar 2000 years and Kaliyuga 1000 years. Each Yuga ends and is preceded by a Sandhyansha. One cycle of four Yugas make one Yuga of the gods.[1]

Seventy one divine Yugas of the gods make one Manvantara. Brahma's one day contains 14 Manus. Each Manavantara has its specified Manu, gods, Indra and the seers[2].

Ceremonies: There are sixteen ceremonies that a Hindu Grihastha (family man) should perform, which include Garbhadhana, Pursavana, Jaat karma, Annaprashana (i.e. from conception to the child's first eating cereal), Mundana (tonsure), Yagyopaveeta (sacred thread), Vivaha (marriage) and lastly the Mritaka Sanskara (last rites) etc. The name giving ceremony should be performed on the 10th, 12th, 30th day after the birth. For this the ideal Muhurta should be found out by consulting the astrologers. The name of a Brahmin should be linked with auspicious meaning, of the Kshatriya with the meaning revealing bravery, of the Vaishya revealing prosperity and of the Shoodra revealing general welfare. For example a Brahmin boy's name could be Vishwakarma, a Kshatriya's Indra Varma, of the Vaishya Dhanavardhan and of the Shoodra like Sarvadas. The names of the female child must conform to the gender and be auspiciously meaningful like Sumangala, Kamala, Supriya etc. The Annaprashana of the child should be held on the

---

1. Please read more about these time division units in our Vishnu Purana of the same series.
2. For greater details see our 'Narada Purana' of the same series.

12th day preferably while the Yagyopaveeta Sanskara should be done before eight years for a Brahmin child, eleven years of the Kshatriya child and 16th year of a Vaishya child. An unmarried Brahmin must wear a Yagyopaveeta of three threads but after marriage it should be of six threads. The Brahmin must study Vedas till they enter the Grahastha Ashram. A student, no matter which caste he belongs to, must avoid contact with woman during the Brahmacharya Ashrama. During the student life (Brahmacharya period) a student should live a hard life. He shouldn't sleep on couches or cushioned mattresses but on the floor. He must serve his guru with total honesty and sincerity and fill his belly by begging food after seeking permission from his guru. He should go for begging to any house only after the sun has crossed mid heaven. The following houses are forbidden for him to get food in begging from: his guru's house or family his own family and from the house of his Gotra[1] members.

After telling about the duties of a 'Batuka' Sumantu told Raja Shatanika about the women with auspicious and inauspicious symptoms.

The Types of Women

Once telling about the physical attributes of women Brahma ji had said that "fortunate are those women who have their sole of feet like the red lotus. Those with dry, half floor touching soles are singularly unfortunate as they get only poverty and distress. Those having toes very close to each other enjoy kingly opulence. Those with toes joints quite pronounced get good ornaments to wear. Those with toe nails slightly reddish and shining get all the pleasures of life. Those who have hard bristles on the outer thighs are generally strife-loving and cantankerous. Those with crow-like thighs are very garrulous and they often suffer widowhood.

Those with knee joints formed like that of a lion or a cat are fortunate. They get male issues. But those who

---

1. Gotra : It literally means the cowpan one gets one's milk supply from. But now in general use it means the clan one's family belongs to,

have excessively shining knees are generally women of easy virtue. The ladies who have much bristles on their body are not desirable as their excessive libido ends up consuming their husband's vitality. However, those with golden-hued soft bristles are bestowers of immense sexual pleasures. The women with an elephant's trunk like softly tapering thighs are by nature sexually overcharged. Those with a vagina having a mole and its opening like the foot of cow enhance poverty of their partner. Those with Kaith-flower like vaginal opening and heavy, sprawling hips are adorable even for the kings. Those with soft, solid and well formed breasts give birth to very fortunate kings. Those with protruding stomach, suppressed pelvic mound and thin buttocks are debauch by nature.

The woman who has during the first pregnancy the right breast a bittle more swollen than the left beget a male issue but those with the left breast more swollen beget a female issue. Those who have their nipple-point bigger than normal with the dark round also wider are cunning and sexually overcharged.

Those women who have the breast region rather fleshless are unfortunate and they are destined to suffer widowhood. Those who have their breast-region rather widespread love their spouse with much of strife and dissension. Theirs is invariably love-hate relationship with their spouse. The lady who has four prominent veins visible on their arm enjoy much love from her spouse. The women with sharp conical hands and soft skin are generally deft in love-plays. Those with dry hands love dissension and they are cantankerous by nature. Those that have whorls on their fingers enjoy good prosperity. If the ladies have three uncut bracelets on their wrist are unable to enjoy pleasure for long.

A woman devoted to the service of her husband is called a Sati. If such a lady keeps fast on the third lunar day (bright) and ends it with a saltless diet, after her death, by virtue of the blessings from Bhagwati Gauri, enjoys beatitude for a long period in heaven. Quoting Bhagwati Uma the Purana says that "if a man also keeps this fast (on the third lunar day of every month during the bright fortnight) he gets a woman of his choice for sure. Such a pair would enjoy eternal bliss like I am enjoying."

He who keeps fast on the fourth lunar day without eating any food and donates sesame seeds to the Brahmins—this he must do for at least two years—enjoys the favour of Lord Shree-Narayan ensuring prosperity of every kind.

Importance of Vratas

During the conversation, Raja Shatanika asked as to what made Lord Ganesh earn the epithet of Lord of Obstructions. "Who had he disturbed as much as to get this title of Vighneshwara?"

Replying to this question Sage Sumantu said: "Once Lord Ganesh had created disturbance in the vow kept by a devout devotee named Gangeya. Kartikeya, the elder brother of Ganesh, felt so much enraged at this disturbance that in his anger he had broken one tusk from Ganesh's visage. When Lord Shiv had asked the reason behind Kartikeya's so much anger, Kartikeya explained: "O Lord, you are called Kapali only because you carry a Kapali (skull) in your hands. But you had thrown it once into the sea. Then the sea had said that he who created any disturbance in once's performance of the Vrata would suffer its consequences. Only when the Vrata is performed religiously that this charge may become ineffective."

[The text of Bhavishya Purana is quite confused here. Suffice it to say that Lord Ganesh earned the epithet of Vighneshwara when he tried to disturb the Vrata of a devotee and Kartikeya had a fight with him on this count.]

To attain one's desires through the favour of the gods, humans can observe certain religious rites called Vratas or vows; periodical fasts called 'Upavasa' and donate alms. This Purana lays much emphasis on Vratas and Upavasas.

A Vrata is a holy resolve either to give up some activity or to follow some specific ritual regularly on certain days or at certain intervals of time.

Before observing a Vrata, one should follow certain preliminaries so as to purify oneself. One should rise early on that day, thoroughly cleanse oneself, offer flowers, fruits, incense and food to the idol and donate alms to Brahmins. One should—in certain Vratas—observe silence throughout the day on which the Vrata is to be followed, control one's temper and check one's passions.

Vratas owe their origin to sages and gods. It is they who instructed mankind to observe these religious rites in order to attain their aims. Subsequently, individuals who benefited from the observance passed on their significance to later generations.

2

Stories Highlighting The Efficacy Of The Vratas

The following stories, culled from the Bhavishya Purana, highlight the efficacy of observance of the Vratas:

The Importance of the Budhashthami Vrata

Once upon a time, in the city of Mithila, there lived a woman called Urmila. She had a son and a daughter. Since she found it difficult to make her living in Mithila, she decided to try her luck elsewhere. Moving away with difficulty, escorting her son and daughter, she reached the city of Avanti and began to do some menial job at a Brahmin's house. She worked very devotedly but she couldn't make the two ends meet. Her children used to starve. Once they were so hungry that Urmila had no way but to steal some grains of wheat from her master's granary. This was how she continued to survive. Meanwhile her daughter Shyamala grew up into a nubile girl of ravishing beauty. She was so beautiful that Yama desired to marry her. Eventually she was married to the death god.

After marriage Yama told Shyamala. "Dear! You are my wife and you are free to roam everywhere in my realm. However there are seven sections (rooms) which are not accessible for you. In fact no mortal can enter them. They are beyond your reach. You should never try to enter them under any condition. You must never attempt to unlock these seven rooms." Shyamala promised to do so. While living in Yama realms she was allowed to visit her mother's place. After a few years, her mother Urmila breathed her last.

While staying in Yama's realms she never attempted to reach the forbidden sections. Once she was getting bored and out of sheer curiosity she exceeded her range and tried to visit those sections (rooms).

When she opened one of the doors and peered into the room, she was shocked to see whatever was there. She saw that, inside the room, Yama's servants were in the process of forcing her mother Urmila into a cauldron boiling with oil. It was too much for her to bear. Unable to bear the sight, Shyamala closed the door and opened the door to another room. In the second room, she found her mother being crushed on a grindstone. Horrified by the sight, Shyamala closed this door and opened the door to the third room. In this room she beheld nails were being driven into her mother's forehead. In the fourth room she beheld her mother, Urmila, was being torn to pieces and the pieces were being thrown before the hungry, fierce-looking dogs.

In fact in all the seven rooms whatever she beheld made her shudder with a dreadful nausea. 'Why is my mother being tortured in such a way after her death? What crimes or crime did she commit?' I always found her to be honest and god fearing", and she couldn't imagine Urmila indulging in any such crime.

At last she went before her husband, the death-god, and confessed her crime of treading into the forbidden rooms. Yama was quite angry: "You have, indeed, been disobedient since I had clearly forbidden you to ever even peep into those sections. As for your mother, she is only being meted out the punishment she deserves. She had committed one serious crime."

"What is that?" Shyamala couldn't help asking.

"Once she had stolen some wheat from the Brahmin who had been her master. You must be aware that stealing any property of a Brahmin is a sacrilege. One who steals from the house of a Brahmin has to suffer in hell till almost eternity. She has to remain there until she completes the divine sentence."

"But this is too much, Lord," Shyamala pleaded. She remembered that once her mother did steal some wheat grain to feed her and her brother. She was sorry for seeing her mother suffering the dire consequences of having done something without any selfish interest. Shyamala again said: "I cannot bear to see my mother suffering such tortures in hell. Can't I do something to relieve her from this deadly consequence? How can I do something to lessen her agony?"

The death-god, Yama, consulted his records and said: "There is one great punya that you had earned. In your previous birth you observed the 'Budhashthami Vrata' as many as eight times. You have still much credit for your meritorious deed. It still vests with you as its efficacy has not yet exhausted itself. In case you agree to transfer that 'punya' to your mother's credit, she may be rescued from the hell."

[The religious rite or Vrata performed on the 8th day of the bright lunar half of every month, as also on the eighth lunar day of the dark half of the particular month Bhadrapada[1], is called the Ashthami Vrata. Should it fall on Wednesday it becomes all the more efficacious. Then it is called Budhashthami Vrata.]

Shyamala readily agreed to transfer that part of her merit to her mother. With the result, Urmila was not only relieved from hell but she earned a permanent nook in heaven in her rejuvenated form. Such is the efficacy of this Vrata whose even indirect effect can release one from the tortures of hell. Those who observe this Vrata are beyond the reach of the Yamadoota according to this Purana.

The Vrata on Shukradwadashi

It is also a very sacred Vrata. If the lunar day 'Dwadashi' falls on a Friday, it is called 'Shukradwadashi Vrata'.

The Purana tells this story to glorify the merit accruing to the performer due to this Vrata.

Once a Brahmin was passing by Vidisha city in the peak of summers when he found a ghostly figure crying in pain and writhing on the banks of the river Vetravati. The sands were truly incinerating and that existence was being invisibly forced to keep lying on those sands. There were boils all over the ghost's body and he was crying for a drop of water. The Brahmin felt pity and he asked: "Why don't you get away from the sands? Why are you torturing yourself this way?"

---

1. This Ashthami of Bhadrapada is included among the 'Ashthami' Vratas because of Lord Krishna's birth on this day.

"O noble Brahmin", that ghostly figure replied, "I am not doing this out of my own volition. What you don't see are the messengers of Yama who are holding me to these smouldering sands. It is a part of punishment that I am being subjected to for my misdeed in my previous life." "What sin did you commit in that life?" Then the ghost told his story given below:

He was a trader (Vaishya class) in his previous life. His name was Shailbhadra. He lived in the city of Vidisha. Despite his being very rich and affluent and having a small family, he never donated anything and enjoyed his wealth in the company of his close relations. Not only that, he never worshipped gods. Since he did nothing good for any one other than his close family members, he couldn't earn any merit. On the contrary, he committed a sin of not helping any needy outsiders or Brahmin. He never donated anything nor served the cow. With the result, after death he was forced to undergo that punishment: "I am being roasted on these burning sands for that sin. O great soul! I cannot bear this agony any more. Please help me."

The Brahmin really felt very sorry for that ghost. He said: "I observed Shukradwadashi Vrata ten years ago. That 'punya' which I earned may help this ghost to get relieved from these tortures."

As he said, the ghost stopped writhing in pain. He smiled and rose high to heaven on account of the merit of observing the Shukradwadashi Vrata getting transferred to his account by that noble Brahmin.

This Purana claims that such holy Vratas have their noble results not only for the performer but also for those whose affection the performer earns.

It lists more such Vratas which are given below:

Ubhaya Dwadadshi: This Vrata, like other Dwadashi Vrata already described, is observed on both the Dwadadshis (of the bright as well as the dark fortnights) and it gives the performer same merit (Punya) as may be received by visiting the holy teerthas as pious as Gaya, Pushkara, Varanasi and Prayaga.

Tilaka Vrata: The observance of a tilaka vrata involves wearing a 'Tilaka' (caste-mark upon one's forehead). This could be an every day feature. It is believed that enemies and evil spirits flee when they see the 'Tilaka' on the forehead of a devotee.

Jatismara Vrata: As has already been explained, a Jatismara means a being who remembers the events of his or her past lives. Its observance requires silence till the moon rises. On this day different gods have to be simultaneously worshipped. A person who faithfully observes this particular religious rite is blessed with this gift.

There are certain Vratas whose even the knowledge of the vidhi (procedural instruction) can get one the 'punya' as effective as almost performing the Vrata. Some of these extra sacred vratas are given below:

(i) **Rasakalyani Vrata:** It was a Vrata which was first observed by Goddess Parvati. In the observance of the Vrata her idol is to be bathed in pure ghee (clarified butter) and worshipped. A person who listens to the Vidhi of this Vrata or persuades others to do the same gets to live in Parvati's realm as all his or her sins are immediately forgiven.

(ii) **Ardranandakari Vrata**. It involves the worship of Shiv and Parvati. One who listens to the 'Vidhi' for this Vrata or makes others do the same gets a place in Indra's abode.

(iii) **Mandarashastithee Vrata**: One who reads out or listens to the 'Vidhi' of 'Mandarashastithee Vrata' is absolved of all sins. The Purana doesn't mention the specific month for this Vrata. Obviously it means that the Vrata is to be performed on all the sixth lunar dates ('Shashthees').

Emphasising on the efficacy of the 'Vratas', this Purana warns that they ought to be performed with total faith and devotion. For if they are performed half-heartedly, they arouse the wrath of the gods. It says that if such displeasure has, indeed, been caused, the wrath of the gods can be appeased by observing the Akhanda-Dwadashi Vrata which involves dedicated worship of Vishnu with offerings and chanting of the Mantra: OM NAMO BHAGWATE VASUDEVAYA.

It is prescribed that certain Vratas are meant to be observed only by women. For example, women can get the 'punya' obtained by men by observing the Ashwamedha Yagya if they dedicatedly observe 'Ananta-Tritiya Vrata' in winters. In observing it it is incumbent upon the married women to wear red clothes while the widows the yellow hued clothes. The unmarried women (girls) should wear only white clothes. On this day women must worship Vishnu and Lakshmi and feed the Brahmins while giving them alms in donation.

Some Vratas Dedicated to the Sun God

This Purana lays special emphasis on observing Vratas dedicated to the sun god. Some of them are listed below:

(i) **Ubhaya[1] Paksha Saptami Vrata:** Observed on the seventh lunar day (saptami) the sun god is worshipped and Brahmins are fed in the winter month of Pousha (roughly December-end). Performed with total dedication this Vrata rewards the observer with the fulfilment of his/her desires for achieving all the four human goals, viz Dharma (righteousness), Artha (wealth), Kaam (fulfilment of all the desires) and Moksha (salvation or the final release).

(ii) **Shukla Paksha Abhaya Saptami Vrata:** This Vrata is observed during the bright fortnight when the seventh lunar date occurs. It is particularly of added significance when it occurs during the month of Shravan. The Vrata performance is rewarded by the sun god by allowing the performer to dwell in his realms or Surya loka.

(iii) **Ananta Saptami Vrata:** This rite is observed on the seventh lunar day during the month of Bhadrapada in the bright fortnight. The reward is a permanent nook in the Surya loka.

(iv) **Bhadrapada Vratas:** The Saptami date (in dark as well as in bright fortnights) is accorded much significance by this Purana. The Vratas should be observed by bathing the image of the sun god in Gangajal and rubbed with clarified butter. The various Vratas are called Kamala Saptami, Kamala Shashthi, Mahasaptami, Mahajaya Saptami, Mahashwetadityavaana Vrata, Martand Saptami Vrata, Ubhaya Saptami Vrata, etc. All these have the common rituals as explained above. [Among these, the Saptami Vrata (during the bright fortnight) and a few Shashtee Vratas still survive].

---

1. 'Ubhaya' literally means both. It means here the Saptami of both the fortnights.

(v) **Durgandha Nashaka Vrata**[1]: This is a peculiar Vrata whose ultimate award is to eliminate foul body odour. Trees preferred by Surya (like the Shami tree and the Banyan) should be worshipped. The date specified for this Vrata is Saptami of Jyestha Shukla Paksha (roughly in the middle of June).

(vi) **Hridayaadityavaana Vrata**: According to other mythological accounts, it was in Vaishaka (April end) that Lord Ram, on the advice of the Sage Agastya, had worshipped Lord Sun and sought his blessings to kill Ravana. It is performed, like other sun-propitiating Vratas, by worshipping the rising sun and keeping fast till the sun-set. The reward is the achievement of worldly desires.

[The Vratas whose details are not supplied by this Purana include Jaya Vrata, Jaya Saptami Vrata, Kamada Vrata etc. In enumerating these Vratas there are repetitions galore.]

(vii) **Mandar Shashti Vrata**: This is observed on the sixth lunar day of the bright fortnight of the month of Margsheera. The sun god is worshipped with the flowers of Mandar (coral tree). If observed properly with all rituals this Vrata's reward is birth in a good family in the next life.

(viii) **Sharkara Saptami Vrata**: Observed on the seventh lunar day (bright fortnight) in the month of Ashvini, wearing white clothes is necessary while bathing the sun-god's image with milk. Donating sweet meats or sugar to the brahmanas is the imperative part of its rituals.

(ix) **Sarvartha Saptami Vrata**: Observed in the dark fortnight of the month of Margasheersha on the seventh lunar day, on this day the observer forsakes the use of salt and oil, worships Surya and donates alms to holy Brahmins. Its reward is attainment of heaven.

(x) **Trivarga Saptami Vrata**: This is observed on the bright fortnight's seventh lunar date in the month of Phalguna. Its rewards ensures the observer staying aloof from all the evil persons.

(xi) **Bhadrapada Shukla Paksha Vrata**: This is chiefly

---

1. This Vrata is a flagrant example of the Hindus mixing hygienic necessities with the religious commandments. For June is the worst month—particularly in North India when the body needs utmost care.

recommended for a poor person who wants to become rich. It involves the control of one's senses and anger and worship of the sun god. It is observed in the bright fortnight of the month of Bhadrapada when the asterism Ardra occurs on the seventh lunar day.

(xii) **Ratha Saptami Vrata**: This is observed on the seventh lunar day in the month of Margasheersha, involving the worship of the sun god (Surya) and his charioteer, Aruna, and feeding Brahmins while also donating alms. This enables one to get birth in a better condition in the next life.

(xiii) **Sankranti Vrata**: This is performed at every transition (Sankranti) of the sun which takes place on 14th or 15th of every month. Particularly on Makar Sankranti Day this has additional significance. On this day the sun god is worshipped with great devotion and alms giving, feeding the Brahmins also take place. Observance of the Sankranti Vrata ensures a life with good health.

(xiv) **Rogaahari Vrata**: In it the observer lives on a diet of milk and fruits, sleeps on the bare ground and worships Surya with a variety of flowers. The observance of this Vrata ensures his cure from all diseases.

Apart from these, in fact all the Saptamis (seventh lunar day) are held sacred to the devotees of Lord Sun. [It appears that the seventh lunar day is especially sacred to Lord Sun as Ekadashi is held dear to Lord Vishnu.]

Besides, these Vratas dedicated to Lord Sun, there are other Vratas that are observed for propitiating other gods as well. The prominent ones are listed below.

(i) **Ananta Chaturdashi Vrata**: It occurs on the 14th lunar day of the month of Bhadrapada's bright half. It is believed that this is observed to propitiate 'Ananta' (an epithet of Shesh Nag, the fabled serpent that supports the earth and upon whose coils' couch Lord Vishnu lies). Only frugal diet of fruits and milk is taken with full meal in the evening. Vishnu is also worshipped on this day as Ananta is believed to be a manifestation of Lord Vishnu's powers. This Vrata ensures the observer's progeny proving itself to be versatile. It also ensures fulfilment of one's desires.

(ii) **Bheeshma Panchaka Vrata**: During the bright fortnight of the month of Kartika this Vrata is observed. It is called after the name of Bheeshma, the grand uncle of Kaurava and Pandavas because he was the first to observe it. Liquers, meat and false speech (telling lies) are to be scrupulously avoided and Vishnu is worshipped. In order to get oneself absolved of the sin of killing a Brahmin this Vrata is also observed.

[In fact it means that the Vrata is so efficacious that even the 'brahmahatya' sin is mollified by its observance. Bheeshma had observed it for he thought he might have killed many Brahmins during the Mahabharata war.]

(iii) **Ashoka Vrata**: On this day the deities of vegetation (Moon and Varuna) are propitiated through a ritual worship of the Ashoka tree to eliminate all grief (Shoka) from one's life.

(iv) **Gopada Triteeya Vrata**: This is observed on 'triteeya' (the third day of the lunar fortnight) in the month of Bhadrapada when asterism Poorva-Bhadrapada is rising in the sky. Cows are worshipped; oil, salt and all cooked items are prohibited. This enables the observer to attain Goloka. [Liberally the realm of cows but it is also identified with the realm of Lord Vishnu].

(v) **Govatsa Dwadashi Vrata**: A cow and her heifer are worshipped on Dwadashi (the twelfth lunar day) during Krishna Paksha (dark fortnight) of the month of Kartika. Celibacy is observed and the worshipper sleeps on the bare floor. This also ensures the observer's entry into Goloka.

(vi) **Govinda Dwadashi Vrata**: Observed in the month of Pousha on the twelfth lunar day during the bright fortnight, on this day the cows are fed. The observer also lives on milk and abjures the use of salt.

(vii) **Kukkuti Vrata**: Observed on the Amavasya of the month of Bhadrapada, Shiv and Parvati are propitiated on this day. It is recommended that the Yagyopaveeta should be formally worn. The reward is the observer may be blessed with the health of his progeny.

(viii) **Madhooka Triteeya Vrata**: In the month of Phalguna during the bright fortnight (on treteeya) this vrata is observed to propitiate Goddess Parvati and the tree Madhooka (Bassia Latifolia). It is generally observed by nubile girls so that they may get a good husband.

(ix) **Nagapanchami Vrata**: On the fifth lunar day of the

dark fortnight of the month of Savan (Shravana) this fast is observed. As the very name suggests, on this day the image of a serpent is ritually made on a piece of cloth and it is worshipped. Nagas (serpents) are fed milk. The reward is total safety from snake or reptile-caused disturbance.

(x) **Ulka Dwadashi Vrata**: This is observed on the twelfth lunar day in the month of Margasheersha when Vishnu is reverentially worshipped so as to cure physical disabilities like deafness and dumbness and the dreadful diseases like leprosy.

(xi) **Vinayaka Chaturthi Vrata**: Observed on the fourth lunar day of the bright fortnight of the month of Bhadrapada, on this day the observer eats sesame seeds' preparations and Lord of all obstructions (Vighneshwar) Ganesh is worshipped. This vrata's observance ensures removal of all impediments in one's life.

(xii) **Shanti Vrata**: Observed for general peace on Ekadashi tithis of the bright fortnight of the month of Kartika, this involves worship of Lord Vishnu. On this day no sour or cereal preparation is eaten. [Some versions claim that both the Ekadashis should be included for the observance of this vrata]. This fast is kept for ensuring general peace and happiness in the family.

(xiii) **Saraswati Vrata**: It is observed on the 5th day of the bright fortnight of the month of Phalguna to propitiate the goddess of learning Saraswati so that she may shower her grace to make the observer learned.

(xiv) **Ashoonyashayana Vrata**: The observer periodically fasts for a period of four months and offers sweet and seasonal fruits to different gods. The reward of this vrata is that a couple stays ever united. Obviously it is to be observed by both husband and wife.

(xv) **Aviyoga Triteeya Vrata**: Observed for marital harmony, this vrata is held on the third lunar day (triteeya) during Shuklapaksha in the month of Margasheersha. Although different gods are worshipped, the main emphasis is laid on the ritual worship of Lord Shiv & Parvati.

(xvi) **Vata Savitri Vrata**: This Vrata has special significance. On this day the tree vata (Banyan) is worshipped which signifies long age. Savitri, as we know, was the wife of Satyavan who brought back her husband from the realm of death after defeating the god of death in a battle of wit.[1] This is celebrated during the Shuklapaksha in the month of Bhardrapada on the third lunar day (treteeya). It is generally observed by married ladies desiring long age of their husband.

(xvii) **Akshaya Triteeya Vrata**: Held on the third lunar day of the bright half of the month of Vaishakha, it is a very auspicious day for solemnising marriage. It is believed that a nuptial union made on this day lasts very long. The parents of the bride and bridegrooms observe this vrata by keeping fast till the 'Kanyadaan' ceremony is over.

(xviii) **Skanda Shashtee**: Observed in the bright fortnight of Kartika month, this is the day on which Kartikeya, the elder son of Lord Shiv, is worshipped. On the sixth lunar day the observer should stand in a holy river and offer 'Dadhi-Ghee-Udak' (sweets made from ghee and sugar and offered with curds) to the setting sun. The entire day the observers keep strict fast. Some of the version of this Purana claim that the offering should be made while looking towards south [possibly because Lord Kartikeya's abode is the Kraunch Parvata which is believed to exist in the southern part of India]. There is no casteist restriction and anybody can observe this fast.

Alms-Giving

A religious rite (Vrata) is held incomplete unless it is accompanied by or concluded by alms-giving.

According to this Purana, wealth-property-money, given in donation never goes waste. In fact it is an investment for a better future or next life. Material wealth is of no use after one's death. It is, therefore, well spent if it is given in donation of alms. A healthy body and a long life serve no purpose if they are not put to some benefit to the other, needy persons. Those who don't donate the alms or wealth to Brahmins and in other philanthropic charity, in fact, have curses and misfortunes lying in wait for them. Most of the ills that one suffer in this world are the consequences of not spending one's wealth in the previous life. The

---

1. It is a popular story whose details may be read in the Mahabharata.

conditions of sickness, hunger, want of the bare necessities remind all what they should have done to escape such consequences.

Furthermore, a 'daan' (donation of alms) must always be accompanied by Dakshina[1] (fees). For every yagya (sacrifice or some noble endeavour), 'dana' (donation) and vrata, a commensurate Dakshina is prescribed which has to be paid immediately. Otherwise no ceremony is deemed complete. This Purana says that for any Yagya the Dakshina is gold or silver coins.

Some of the prominent 'Dana' are the following:

(i) **Godana**: It is held to be the most sacred 'Daan'. A healthy cow and calf are donated to a learned, Veda-versed Brahmin. It is believed that such a 'dana' ensures one getting a nook in the heaven following one's death. Even during life one gets all the benefits of a blessed life.

(ii) **Vrishabha Dana**: If an ox is donated as alm, one clears the sins of his seven generations.

(iii) **Mahishee Dana**: The donation of a she-buffalo ensures the fulfilment of one's all worldly desires. But the buffalo ought to be milch.

(iv) **Bhoomi Dana**: Donation of a piece of land is supposed to eradicate all sins.

(v) **Griha Dana**: The donation of a well decorated house is rewarded by one's stay in Lord Shiv's realm.

(vi) **Anna Dana**: Donation of cereal to the hungry and needy makes one stay in Lord Vishnu's realm.

(vii) **Halapanktee Dana**: A plough, made of gold and jewels, with forty models of golden bullocks attached in a line (pankti) to the plough, donated to a Brahmin ensures the donor attaining a place in heaven for a period of seven generations.

(viii) **Apaka Dana**: One thousand utensils are gifted for the attainment of sons, servants and riches.

(ix) **Thali (Sthali) Dana**: A copper or a clay plate (sthali), laden with food, is donated to the hungry Brahmins. Its reward is getting an inexhaustible stock of food by the donor.

---

1. It is a unique feature in this faith that the donor, and not the acceptor of the alms, feels obliged. The fee is the token of that gratefulness.

(x) **Shaiyya Dana**: The gifting of a bed (Shaiyya) to a Brahmin ensures comfort to the soul.

(xi) **Agni Dana**: Particularly during winters placing a well-lit fire in a metal container at a common place so as to give warmth to passerby is called Agni Dana. This almsgiving ensures fulfilment of the donor's worldly desires.

(xii) **Prapa Dana**: A 'prapa' is a stand for providing drinking water to the travellers. In colloquial parlance it is also called a 'Pyaauoo'. A few water-filled pitchers are kept on the way of the travellers under a shady tree during summers. This form of donation is held to be very sacred and its reward is getting a berth in the heavens.

(xiii) **Dasi Dana**: A well decorated maid servant is donated to a Brahmin to ensure the donor enjoying all pleasures during his stay in heaven.

(xiv) **Vidya Dana**: This donation is also held to be very sacrosanct. Providing free education to any one also comes under this category. Gifting a book, a sheet of paper and inkpot to a Brahmin ensures one remaining educated in all the subsequent births.

(xv) **Hiranyagarbha Dana**: The hungry are fed and a golden image is donated to a Brahmin. This too ensures a passage to heaven.

(xvi) **Brahmanda Dana**: A golden egg (an egg-shaped gold-made object) is prepared and golden images of Brahma, Vishnu and Shiv are placed on the egg. The egg is then donated to a Brahmin, together with corn, shoes and an umbrella. This erases sin and realises one's objectives. [Normally this gift is a part of the 'dana' made immediately after one's death by his descendants.]

(xvii) **Tula Dana**: Normally this is done by the parents on their child's birthday so as to ensure the child enjoying all riches in life. 'Tula' is a pair of scales. The child is made to sit in one of the scales and the other is laden with gold, silver, cereals, salt, to the extent that both the scales are evenly balanced. Half of the alms thus donated is given to the Brahmins, one-fourth to the priest who aided in the ceremony and one-fourth to the needy ones. This 'dana' also ensures not only the child's rich life but also much comfort after his quitting his mortal coil.

(xviii) **Kalpavriksha Dana**: Kalpavriksha is that fabled

tree that fulfils one's desire merely by asking. This donation is symbolical of this kind of alms-giving in which a golden tree with golden fruit is constructed and donated to a Brahmin. The reward is dwelling in the realm of Surya with all comforts.

(xix) **Saptasagar Dana**: Saptasagar is symbolical of gifting some amount of salt, milk, jaggery and sugar are donated to Brahmin so as to have all previous sins erased.

(xx) **Dhanya Parvata Dana**: Mounds of grain are donated along with the gift of jaggery, gola and clarified butter to Brahmin. This is specially done on the day of Annakoota which falls just after the Diwali festival.

(xxi) **Punya Dana**: This is a symbolical alms-giving. In it the person, with a definite resolution, prays god to transfer the 'Punya' to his credit to the other person—whom he mention by name and family—so that the other person may also be absolved of his or her sin.

The Caste System

This Purana emphasises that the caste system devised by Manu should be followed for social peace. In fact each Purana discusses this system and avers its adherence. But this Purana, i.e. Bhavishya Purana, is less rigid than what other Puranas assert. As is well known, it has four categories of persons in a society. The Brahmins should have their prime aim in learning and sacrifice. They are the ones who have the responsibility of guarding a society from the morality point of view. The Kshatriyas are the defenders from any aggression and it is their job to maintain law and order in the society. The main job of the Vaishyas is practising trade and agriculture and that of the Shoodra is to serve the other three sections of society and maintain cleanliness.

However, the Bhavishya Purana is emphatic that birth by no means is the sole determinant of the caste of the person. It cites the examples of the high sages like Parashara, Shukadeva, Vashishtha, Mandapala and others who rose above their lowly origins. The same is the case of Sage Vishwamitra who was a born Kshatriya but attained Brahmanahood by dint of his penance and prayers. But it also states that a Chandala (a pariah or an outcaste) or a

Shoodra, though he might study the Vedas by fraud or by going out of the country, cannot, by mere study of the Vedas, become a Brahmin.

This Purana unambiguously asserts that it is one's conduct and not the study of the Vedas or Sanskaras (holy rituals) that makes a man a Brahmin in the true sense of the term. Of course it is true that the study of the Vedas is the professional duty of Brahmins but it is the inherent character of the person that identifies one as a Brahmin. No amount of the Veda learning can save a person who has deviated from the path of the righteous conduct. The teaching of the Vedas must percolate down to the person's conduct conforming to the basic traits of a Brahmin.

The Bhavishya Purana further says that a Shoodra and a Brahmin—at their birth—have only difference of name as there is nothing distinct or any distinguishing factor between them. Both are just human beings. According to this Purana, Shoodras are not debarred from wearing the sacred thread or from praying. No matter what they do, it is the basic, inherent character that makes a man Brahmin—not his observance of a few rituals or chanting of the mantras.

Nevertheless there are certain acts or profession which a Brahmin shouldn't indulge in if he wants to retain his Brahminhood. Those Brahmins who graze cows, goats or sheep and who become servants, shopkeepers and blacksmiths lose their Brahminhood. Certain kinds of food are also forbidden for the Brahmin class. They should not eat or sell meat, garlic and onions, drink liquor or the milk of camels. They shouldn't accept food at the time of a birth or a death. Food habits together with one's profession distinguish one class from other. Apart from these a Brahmin must maintain a moral dignity and eschew back-biting. Not only should he practise high moral standard but should inspire others as well.

The Bhavishya Purana categorically says that one's class is not absolutely immutable or predetermined. A Shoodra can become a Brahmin and vice-versa. Similarly a Kshatriya can become a Vaishya and the converse is also possible. The special powers that a Brahmin acquries through the Mantras are also acquireable by a Shoodra. He can also develop powers through his penance and discipline that his cause may also become as efficacious as it may be if uttered by a Brahmin. Should a member of the higher class deviate from the ordained path of his group, he can always slide down the social rung. No individual can retain his class if he does not fulfil the duties that have been prescribed for his class. Hence it is apparent that this class diversion is not or never has been based on the vagaries of birth. Even if one is a born Brahmin with all the refinement through the Sanskaras, yet he indulges in the vile act like stealing, kidnapping, dacoity etc. not only he will go to hell, he will be tortured there much more painfully than a Shoodra, should the latter commit the same crime. And if there be a Shoodra who is honest, devoted to his duties, doesn't indulge in vice-practices, let above the society even after his death he would get a better realm—so declares this Purana.

The view held by other Puranas was that some consideration in this caste division also included the complexion of the person. But this Purana is critical of the view that Brahmins are white like the moon, Kshatriyas are red like the 'Kinshuka' flower, Vaishya are yellow like the 'haritala' (yellowish mineral colour like orpiment) and Shoodras are black like coal. Such complexion based distinction is not true as any member of any class could have any complexion.

As a matter of fact, the Bhavishya Purana goes to question the very basis of the 'Varna-Vyavastha.' It says that like sons of the same father, like fruits of the same tree, all Brahmins, Kshatriyas, Vaishyas and Shoodras have the same constituent elements. They cannot be differentiated on the basis of any physical quality like complexion or general appearance. They all belong to the same species and not as visibly different as a cow or a horse from each other.

There is no doubt that by the time this Purana was compiled, the influence of other races had started to tell upon the Indian society. Hence it seemingly incorporated some fresh ideas on the subject of class or caste distinction. Since it seems to include as belated Indian history as the advent of even the British, the absorption of different races must have reduced the distinctions in the general appearance of the caste to the minimum. May be the indirect influence of the 'class-less' faiths like Christianity and Muslims, the Bhavishya Purana made this distinction of speaking almost against the Varna Vyavastha.

It was not that the Varna Vyavastha was prevalent only in the Indian society. The Bhavishya Purana claims that the population of Shakadvipa was grouped into four classes called Maga, Magaga, Ganaga and Mandaga or Mandhabha, who were equivalent to Brahmins, Kshatriyas Vaishyas and Shoodra of the Hindu casteist system.

According to ancient Iranian books they had Maga Brahmins, and the entire society was divided into four sections or layers (pishtras): Atharvas (priests), Kathaesthas (warriors), Vastriyas (family chiefs) and 'buitlis' (labourers).

The Earth and Its Regions

Like other Puranas, the Bhavishya Purana also states that the earth is divided into seven regions (dweepa) and their names are Jambudweepa, Plakshadweepa, Shalmaladweepa, Kushadweepa, Kraunchadweepa, Pushkardweepa and Shakadweepa.

While Bharatavarsha[1] is in Jambudweepa, Persia (Iran) is said to be in Shakadweepa.

[In Iran and the round about region there used to be strictures againt a man's aspiring for a position higher than what society had allotted to him at the time of his birth. But there was also considerable freedom of movement from one class to another. May be the Iranian influence, brought by the Persian, had influenced the Indian caste system.]

The Bhavishya Purana says that Shakadweepa surrounds the ocean that is known as 'Dadhi Samudra' or ocean of curds.

It says the cities of Shakadweepa are clean and the inhabitants have long lives. Famine, disease and old age were unknown in that land. There were seven snowy-white mountains in the region and these mountains abounded in

---

1. 'Varsha' literally means a large chunk of space of time. Hence 'Bharat varsha' means a large chunk of Jambudwaka of Bharat.

precious stones. Jewels were also be found in the seven rivers that flew through the country.

The fabled mountain called Meru, according to this Purana, is located in Shakadweepa. This was where the sages and Gandharvas lived. The second mountain, which leaned slightly to the east, was called Udaya, with a golden peak. Clouds gathered here in great number. The third mountain was called Mahagiri. It abounded in lakes. It was from these lakes that Indra collected the water that was (is) used for creating the clouds. Mahagiri was a vastly populated region. The fourth mountain was called Raivataka. Exactly above it was (and is) the Nakshatra called Revati. The mount, in fact, derived its name from this asterism. This mountain was called the heaven of Shakadweepa. The fifth mountain was named Shyama and it was dark in colour. The sixth mountain was Antagiri and it was argent in hue. The seventh and the last mountain, according to this Purana, is Ambikeya. This is always covered in show and is practically inaccessible.

Like Jambudweepa[1] is called so because of the abundant growth of this tree (Jamuna) in the region, the same way Shakadweepa is called so because of the abundant growth of the 'Shaka' tree.

According to Bhavishya Purana there are seven sacred rivers in Shakadweepa. They are held so holy that each of them is referred to as the Ganga, although they have individual names as well. They are called Shivajala or Anutapta, Kumari or Vasavi, Nanda or Parvati, Shivitika or Parvati, Ikshu or Kratu, Dhenuka or Mrita and the Ganga (Its individual name is not given). All these rivers flow into ocean. Their waters are very clean, holy and entirely thirst-quenching.

The Purana lists four classes of the Shakadweepa which have already been given. These inhabitants are extremely religious. They do not suffer from hatred, jealousy and sorrow. These inhabitants are generally sun worshippers. They worship the most luminous god through Vratas and fasts.

---

1. Since the details of Jambudweepa have been repeatedly given in other Puranas, for paucity of space, they are being omitted here.

The Sun-Worshippers

There are three classes of followers or worshippers of Surya, according to the Bhavishya Purana, which suggests them to have come from Shakadweepa mostly. They were sun-worshipping Magas, the fire-worshipping Magas and the sun-worshipping Bhojakas. According to this Purana the letter 'ma' is the symbol of the sun god. One who meditates on 'ma' is called a Maga. A Maga is thus a sun-worshipper. The sun or Surya is the supreme god of the Magas. They cook their meals for the sake of the sun and eat only after praying to the sun. They belong originally to Shakadweepa which is located beyond Jambudweepa.

The Story of Shamba

Lord Krishna married Jambavati and their union had produced a son named Shamba. Shamba was a delinquent boy and as a curse imposed on him by his father, Shamba contracted leprosy[1]. Shamba was told that his leprosy would be cured if he worshipped the sun. He constructed a temple dedicated to the sun on the banks of the river Chandrabhaga (Chenab). Since the priests of Shakadweepa were well versed in the worship of Surya, Shamba invited them to come and act as priests at the temple that he had built.

Maga Priests

The peculiarity of these Maga sages was that they took their meals in total silence. Normally even ordinary people from Shakadweepa also kept silence at meal times. These Maga Brahmins wore a sacred thread, known as the 'Avyanga' around their waists. They grew beards and never touched carcasses and other unclean objects. The Bhavishya Purana claims that these Maga Brahmins kept their mouths covered as a protection against uncleanliness. [Perhaps their influence reflected upont the Jain seers.] They had a special emphasis on donating their earnings. They generally ate fruits and vegetables as part of their diet.

How these Maga Brahmins came into being is given in the form of a story in the Purana.

---

1. For details read The Bhagwata Purana of the same stories.

Maga Brahmins' Birth

Once upon a time there was a sage called Rijivha. He was an ardent devotee of the fire-god, Agni. He had a daughter named Nikshubha[1]. Surya (the sun-god) secretly married her and their union produced a son called Jarashabda. Since Nikshubha had married the sun-god secretly without letting her father know about it, Rijivha was greatly angered. Despite his ardent love for his daughter he cursed her: "I curse you that your son would be a rogue, an unworthly existence."

Nikshubha was very much worried. She prayed to the sun-god who quietly appeared before her. "Although I cannot overrule your father's curse," he said, "as he is a reputed sage, yet I bless your son to have descendants well versed in the Vedas. They would wear the sacred thread, known as 'Avyanga'. This way no matter your son to be proving unworthy his descendants will be quite noble and renowned."

It was these descendants of Jarashabda who came to be known as Maga Brahmins. They were the ardent devotees of the sun-god. The Purana also says that some of his descendants also worshipped the fire-god, Agni.

[It is quite obvious that the Magas of this Purana were the Magi priests of ancient Persia. Scholars believe their migration to India having taken place during the period of the Kushanas. Although 'Iran' is not worded as it is in this Purana, Shakadweepa is generally said to be the ancient Indian name for Persia or Iran. The Parsi community which appears to be constituted by their descendants is still the worshippers of the fire-god and the sun-god. What is similar between the Bhavishya Purana and the Iranian sacred book 'Avesta' (Zend-Avesta) is their referring to five kinds of fire (Agni). Moreover phonetically Jarashabda and Zarathushtra appear not much apart, given the pronunciational difference of the two regions. The Parsis who are said to be descendants of the ancient Iranians wore a sacred thread which they call 'Avoyonhava' which is also not much dissimilar with the term quoted in this Purana, 'Avyanga'.

---

1. In some accounts Nikshubha is identified with Chhaya, the second wife of the sun-god.

It is quite clear from the above comparisons that Bhavishya Purana must have been compiled much later than the other celebrated Puranas like the Vishnu Purana or Devi Bhagwat Purana. So much of the foreign influence—apart from Iranians' migrations this Purana also refers about the British advent to India—clearly indicates it to have been compiled in the latter part of the 17th century AD. Hence its covering all these details].

Like the Magas even the Bhojakas also appear to have migrated from Shakadweepa. They were the sun-worshippers. But there are differences between them.

While the Bhojakas made daily offering of food (bhojana) to Surya, along with incense, garlands and other gifts, this is not the case with the Magas. The Bhojakas must study the Vedas, bathe thrice a day, pray to the sun-god five times a day[1] and refuse food from a Shoodra. A Bhojaka should wear the sacred thread 'Avyanga' at all times, as only when he wears it that he attains purity and receives the sun-god's blessings. A Bhojaka is not entitled to worship the sun-god if he is not wearing the sacred thread. The Purana says that if a bhojaka gives up the sacred thread, he loses good health and he may be deprived of having any progeny—thus he cannot attain heaven. The Purana says that the sacred thread represents all that is good in life—the godly influence, purity, noble ideas and love for all beings. The end of the sacred thread, where the knot is tied to make it the thread of consecration, is generally called 'Sumeru'. The three threads represent Brahma, Vishnu and Mahesh.

The Purana gives the impression as though the Bhojakas had come to attain a higher status than the Magas. This Purana praises the sense of devotion of the Bhojaka in the superlative terms. It says that as a wife serves her husband, a pupil his perceptor, so the Bhojakas serve the sun-god. Just as there is no sacred text equal to the vedas, no river equal to the holy Ganga, no Yagya equal to the Ashwamedha Yagya (the horse sacrifice), no pleasure equal to the birth of a son and no god equal to the sun-god, there is no devotee equal to the Bhojakas before the sun-god. So much so,

---

1. This five-time worship schedule in a day reminds perhaps the Muslim influence upon them or vice-versa.

that according to this Purana the deeds of the Bhojakas should be treated as being performed by the great Surya himself. In fact, according to this Purana the Bhojakas are the most holy Brahmin and it claims that for attaining final release one has to attain the status of a Bhojaka.

The Tale About the Bhojakas

Swayambhoo Manu had one son named Priyavarta. It was Priyavarta who built a temple dedicated to the sun-god. He installed a golden idol of Lord Surya in the temple. But despite his best attempt Priyavarta could not get a suitable priest capable of performing the ritual worship of the god at the temple. He thought as though the temple would become useless as there was no one who could perform the worship of Lord Sun in a desired way. He grew desperate and in his nervousness he started praying to Lord Sun feelingfully. Pleased with his prayer, Lord Sun appeared there and said:

"What boon do you seek, son?" the Lord asked. "Please grant me the boon that there may be many priests at this temple to render you a devoted worship."

"Let it be so", and saying so the sun-god created eight men out of his own body. Two had been born from the forehead, two from the arms, two from the legs and two from the rays of the sun.

These eight men were the forefathers of the Bhojakas and they were made the priests of the temple in Shakadweepa.

Yet another temple was also created at the southern bank of the river Yamuna[1] by Samba, the grandson of Lord Krishna.

---

1. Yamuna is generally the name given to any river's main tributary. Hence it may not be the Yamuna passing from Mahura.

3

Education, Marriage And Temples

The Bhavishya Purana gives vivid description of the types of education available upto the period it was compiled in.

(a) **Education**: Comparing education—gain with water—procurement it says that a student obtains knowledge after serving his teacher (guru) faithfully the same way we obtain water after digging a well. His completion of education is symbolised by his presenting to his guru the Dakshina' comprising land-piece, gold, an umbrella, footwear, clothes, grain and vegetables. Without this payment the education is held to be incomplete.[1]

A Guru is he who knows the true meaning of the Gayatri (the most sacred Mantra) and who devoutly follows the law ('maryada' or norms) is described as the best of a guru. Moreover, it is the basic duty of a Brahmin to gain and disseminate knowledge. Hence the rule, according to this Purana, that a Brahmin who doesn't fulfil his obligation is not entitled to get a maintenance allowance from the state or by the rest of society. He who doesn't know how to keep

---

1. The hidden idea behind this rule ought to be education. It was a sort of the final test with the teacher writing to ascentain whether his pupil is educated enough to earn his survival independently. If the pupil is able to give prescribed 'Dakshina' it naturally would mean that he is competent enough. And it is not to be paid with other's help. The pupil has to arrange this Dakshina by his own efforts; he couldn't have borrowed it from his parents, friends or well-wisher. This tradition becomes quite pronounced in the Dwapar Yuga where a guru (Dronacharya) was not to be satisfied with his pupil's parent, friend or well-wisher giving his hacked off thumb but only with that of his pupil (Ekalavya) giving it from his person. This hidden logic makes this rule very relevant even in the modern age!

learning is incapable of rendering true education to his pupils. It is because the current of knowledge not held strong tends to go stale and irrelevant.¹

There were five grades of teachers prevalent then:

(i) **Acharya**: The top position, who is able to teach even the most secret knowledge [Kalpa-Rahasya] of the Vedas. In short the most learned person, literally 'knower of all'.

(ii) **Upadhyaya**: He who taught for earning a livelihood was an Upadhyaya.

(iii) **Guru**: A teacher with capabilities to make his pupils stay with him so as to practically prepare them for life. Obviously he is more than a teacher as he is a teacher who provides them boarding and lodging apart from personally instructing them in all rituals. Since it was a very important institution for the society it was headed generally by a Rishi.²

(iv) **Ritvija**: This is one who adopts the performance of sacrifice as a profession.
(In modern parlance this could be an apprentice Rishi.)

(v) **Batuka**: A student of the celebrated school run by a Rishi or a competent person. Loosely it also means a student learning Sanskrit. [This term Sanskrit may also mean refinement.]

(vi) **Mahaguru or Maharshi**: 'Maha' is just a term raising the degree tremendously. He who is versed in not only the existing knowledge but also that which is either in the incipient and decadent stage.

---

1. Again an order worthy of emulation even during the modern time.
2. Literally he who creates bliss but generally, by the standard lexicon meaning: an inspired poet or sage with proven sanctity. This was the category of the erudite scholars who could move the common people by their creative process. It was the Rishi who created 'Richars' (the aphorism of the Vedas to create Bliss). In contrast there were 'Munis' who would brood over these creations and finally recommend them to be practised in life and adopted as the norms of a society. In modern parlance this was the role model for every class and anyone could acquire this position by his perseverance and dedication. While Vishmamitra was a born Kshatriaya he became a Rishi; Vashishtha despite being a born Brahmin could also earn this epithet and not by birth.

He must have the knowledge of all the Scriptures, Neeti Shastra, Nyaya, Darshan as well all the cults adored by the people of an age.

Grades of Payment (Wages): Each one is allowed the payment commensurate with the importance of the job. Obviously a teacher's one hour would be tangibly and tremendously costly than that of a working Shoodra's wages for an entire day.

Varata was the smallest unit of payment. It used to be the cheapest brass-piece coin. Twenty Varatas were supposed to make one 'Kakini and a 'lana' had four 'Kakini' i.e., a 'pana' had eighty Varatas.

According to the Bhavishya Purana the cost of bricklaying (per day) was 2 'Panas', digging a well—two 'Panas'. Sweeping—one Varata, each copper ware's production cost was '4 Panas', of bronze—3 Panas, weaving cloth—3 Panas', wearing wollen cloth—10 Kakinis, a blacksmith's wage was 10 Kakinis, that of a barber—10 Kakini, (only shaving—2 Kakinis and including hair cutting was 10 Kakinis). But hair dressing was decidedly a costly affair—4 Panas. Beauty treatment for women was 1 Pana cost. A carpenter would make a whole (wooden) plough for two Panas. Planting rice was one Pana cost and so was the cost of planting betel nuts and chillies. Pulling a vehicle (as also perhaps of carrying a palanquin, per carrier) was 1 Pana and 10 Varata cost. Even small (wooden) bridges could be constructed in 2 Panas. A stage for any performance could have been made in 1 Pana.

Laying marble floors was, per person, 1 Pana. The laundry charges were: normal sized cloth 1 Pana, for bigger cloths or the woollen one half a 'pana' more, which was also the charge of getting the normal sized cloth urgently laundered.

The Purana is vary specific about having the various stages of life for girls though it also recommends their marriage as early as possible.

(i) **Gauri**: A girl's epithet upto seven years of her age.

(ii) **Nagarika**: A ten-year-old girl, it also means a girl was called so between seven and ten years.

(iii) **Kanya or Kanyaka**: A girl upto twelve years of age.

(iv) **Rajaswala**: Girls older than this age were called

'Rajaswala' (meaning that the process of mensutruation having already commenced in their case).

The Purana says that the best age for one's daughter's marriage is when she is in the Gauri stage. According to it, a menstruating daughter makes the father a sinner. Marriage before puberty is strongly recommended for the girls.

After menstruation, a girl was at liberty to choose her groom. Perhaps this gave rise to the custom of 'Swayamvara'. Once a daughter attains puberty, her father couldn't force her daughter to marry any man or boy of his choice. She had the liberty of having her choice, with the culprit father bearing the cost of the ceremony.

Types of Marriage

Like other Puranas and standard scriptural texts, there are eight forms of marriage which are briefly described below:

(i) **Brahma**: A well dressed bride adorned with all kinds of jewellery is given away in marriage to a learned bridegroom from a noble family, after the bridegroom having been especially invited for the occasion.

(ii) **Daiva**: A well adorned wife is given in marriage to a husband of good conduct. The ceremony of wedding takes place flamboyantly in the presence of the invited guests. The priest conducts the ceremony in which the performance of the sacrifice is a must.

(iii) **Arsha**: Arsha marriage literally means traditional marriage. In it the bride's father gives his daughter away to the bridegroom while instructing the pair to always remain together in the discharge of their religious duties.

(iv) **Prajapatya**: The bride's father gives his daughter away to the bridegroom after performing rites and donating a cow. [Some versions claim the cow donation to have been a part of Aarsha marriage.]

(v) **Asura**: In it the father and his relations give the daughter against the receipt of some kind of money, property and gift.

(vi) **Gandharva**: This is an ancient equivalent of the modern love marriage. A man and a woman falling in love decide to get tied in a nuptial bond without caring for any condition or ritual whatsoever.

(vii) **Rakshasa**: A man abducting a woman and forcing her to surrender herself to his lust without any precondition.

(viii) **Paishacha**. It is only like Rakshasa marriage with the difference that in it the man uses his tricks and deceit to forcibly possess the woman.

According to this Purana the desirable forms of marriage are Brahma, Daiva, Arsha. It is believed that children from such union redeem their ancestors.

After marriage the woman must act like the woman of the house to make it run on the lines suggested by her husband's family. She must owe her loyalty to this family only. She must regard her husband as a god and hence must follow his every order.

Although the Purana asserts that a wife forms half of her husband's body and hence she is 'Ardhangini', it, nevertheless, categorically says that woman should remain subservient to her husband. But since she is half of what her husband is, her neglect means destruction of the half of the house immediately.

The Ideal Woman

Describing the symptoms and the role of an ideal housewife, the Purana says that she must be awake before the stroke of the dawn. Then she must tell the servants their jobs for the day. She must also supervise the work of the servants. In case the servants be not there, she must sort out the work that she must accomplish herself and assign the remaining work to various members of the house. Her primary duty is to keep her husband and other members of the house well-fed. Washing of utensils, preparing and sweeping the floor of the kitchen with fresh cow-dung and keeping it thoroughly clean are some of her duties. Additionally, if she has spare time she must assist her husband in doing outside jobs.

The Purana also prescribes some 'dont's' for a good housewife. She should not sit alone, laugh in the company of strangers, stand at the gate, look in the direction of the main road, talk loudly, walk ahead of people, laugh rather unnecessarily and excessively and exchange house-hold things with her neighbours.

When her husband be not at home, she shouldn't

beautify herself or wear ornaments. She should venture out only when it is rather unavoidable. She must not pass her time in idle pursuits at all and should rush back as soon as the work is over.

During pregnancy she must bathe in scented water, avoid loud laughter and stay away from undesirable people. She must not brood over petty things and avoid being unduly anxious. Also, she must not take any risk whatever during this position.

Curiously enough, the Bhavishya Purana permits divorce if either the husband or the wife is not satisfied or if there is continuous friction between them. In case the wife may be a barren and incapable of giving her husband a male issue, the husband must wait for eight years before taking the divorce. Also, when the divorce is granted because of marital unhappiness, the 'Stree-Dhana' (the jewellery or personal property of the woman) must be duly returned to her. Apart from it she is also entitled to having the subsistence allowance from her husband.

The Bhavishya Purana also makes provision for a person having more than one wife. If there happens to be a co-wife, the younger wife should treat the elder one as a mother and must take care to treat her (co-wife's) children as well. Not only this, whatever she gets from her own home must be offered first to the elder wife. And from her side, the elder wife must accept the younger one as a daughter. The husband must not practise discrimination in such a way as to cause friction and dissension between his two wives.

Planting of Trees and Their Reward: Planting such trees as are shady redeems one's ancestors. A male issueless person must plant such a tree near a temple or any place of worship for having his desire fulfilled. In fact the planting of a Peepal tree absolves one from the false charges very quickly and also makes one ensure final release if one doesn't commit sins. Planting of Ashoka tree eliminates all sorrow that may surround oneself. If one wants a good wife, he must plant a 'Plaksha' tree. The planting of the Jamuna tree fills one's coffers quickly. Tendu-tree's plantation ensures one getting a large, well to do family. If one plants a pomegranate tree one is allowed to enjoy much sensual pleasures. Planting of Bakula and Vanjula tree eliminates one's sins. If one plants 'Valvala', Madhooka and Arjuna tree one gets plenty of property and enjoyment of wealth.

Planting of Shinshipa, Jayanti and Kadamba trees, one reserves a nook for oneself in heaven.

Temples and Icons (Images)

The Bhavishya Purana gives a long list of temples, the images that are to be installed in them and what merit accrues to one by having those temples built. It says—that the act of building a temple is wonderful in that it combines the 'Punya' obtained from performing a sacrifice with the Punya obtained from constructing public works like wells. Those who have the temples constructed ensure for themselves a nook in the heaven.

Since the gods are the images that man conjures up to eke out his shortcomings, the temples are generally made in very picturesque surroundings, amidst lakes, wells, flowers and trees and in places where the melodious notes of birds can be heard. Hence the temple is the piece of art and it need to be constructed with care.

That is the reason why all types of land are not suitable for building temples. Land where objects like hair, bones, coal, lime, husks and similar objects are found are generally rejected as sites for temples. Ground that accepts all kind of seeds is preferred. The ground that makes the sound of a cloud or drum when struck is the ideal choice.

The different 'Varnas' have their individual choice for different types of land. The Brahmins prefer the land with whitish hue while the Kshatriyas choose red earth for building temples, the Vaishya the earth with yellowish hue and the Shoodras the earth with blackish complexion.

The normal procedure is testing the quality of the ground before a temple is built. To conduct this test, a pit should be dug in the earth. The pit should then be refilled with the earth that has been dug out. If the pit is filled and still there is some extra earth that is left over, then the land is held to be of superior quality (Uttama land). The temple can be merrily built over it. If the pit is just filled with no extra earth being left over then the land is held to be of medium quality (Madhyama). Although a temple could be built over the earth, it is not the best place to do so. Similarly the pit is dug and if some empty space remains when the dug earth is filled, it means that the land is of inferior quality and hence 'Adhama' land. Therefore the temple should not be made there.

When a temple is constructed dedicated to Surya-Dev, special care needs to be taken. The gate of the temple should always face the east. In case this could not be possible then the gate should be facing the west. There should be a bathing space (some bathroom or provision for having a water source) south of the main temple. The place for worshipping the fire should be to the north. Temples dedicated to Shiv, Brahma and Vishnu should respectively be erected to the north, the east and the west of the Surya temple. It should be surrounded by the shrines dedicated to minor divinities. This whole complex of the temple is deemed one unit. It must also have a half open place (Veranda) where the Puranas could be recited to the desirous listeners.

As far as offerings are concerned, they should be made from two cupolas (Mandapa). While the cupola on the right should be used making the offerings at sunrise, on the left the cupola should be reserved for making the offering at sun-set.

This Purana quotes the divine architect, Vishwakarma, to say that as many as 3000 different kinds of structures or designs can be used for building temples. The major designs or shape of the temple construction are the following:

(i) **Shadosheersha**: A single storeyed construction with sixteen apices. [Some versions of this Purana call this category Shadoshara meaning a construction with sixteen sides]

(ii) **Padma**: Single-storey, lotus shaped.

(iii) **Meru**: Multi-storeyed with several apices.

(iv) **Kailash**: Multi-storeyed with a single peak.

(v) **Vimanachhanda**: Air-vehicle-like with several sections.

(vi) **Nandana**: A peakless, compact structure.

(vii) **Samudra**: A circular construction with no or single storey.

(viii) **Vritta**: A circular construction with a single storey.
(ix) **Vrisha**: A twin-storeyed circular construction.
(x) **Mrigasimha**: A semi-circular or octagonal shaped construction with only one storey.
(xi) **Garuda**: A bird-shaped (Garuda like) structure with a little peak atop.
(xii) **Nandi**: A construction resembling a bull with two peaks symbolising two horns.
(xiii) **Gajakunjara**: An elephant-back-like construction with two protruding sections.
(xiv) **Guharaja**: A construction resembling a deep cave.
(xv) **Hansa**: With an elliptical base the construction shaped like a swan in flight.
(xvi) **Kumbhaghata**: With a ground plan shaped like a pot.
(xvii) **Sarvato Bhadra**: It is a five-storeyed construction with many apices and a square base.
(xviii) **Chatusra Chatuskona**: A square based single piece construction.
(xix) **Astashara**: An eight-sided single storey construction.

Having outlined these nineteen types of construction, this Purana also throws enough light on the material to be used for making the idols or images with the commensurate rewards. The most favoured idol is that of gold (Kanchana). The second choice is silver (rajata), copper (tamra), earth (mrithika or raw earth), stone (shail), wood (Varkshu) and of Ashthadhatu (using all the eight natural metals which are gold, silver, copper, tin, lead, iron, zinc, mercury).

Building icons with different materials has its commensurate rewards, as this Purana declares. For example the installation of the wooden icons grants long life and riches. The icons of clay grant pleasure in every realm. The icons that are fashioned out of jewels or precious stones grant prosperity in every way. Gold icons give the installer intrinsic strength to enjoy life for long while the silver ones grant fame and copper ones children. Stone image grants landed property.

Even for making wooden icons the astrologers should be consulted about selecting the auspicious time for cutting the wood. It is done as a ceremony. First the 'Muhurta' should be determined for getting the wood and only then the carpenter should be sent to the jungles. The wood selected should be sturdy, and heavy. One should, therefore, avoid cutting thin trees, trees going in temples' land or cremation grounds. Generally selected wood for this purpose are Devadaru (a species of pine), Chandana (sandalwood), Bilva (rose apple which is held to be a dear tree to Lord Shiv), Amra (mango), Nimba (Neem), Panasa (jackfruit) and Raktachandan (red sandalwood).

The Purana gives detailed instructions about building an image of the sun-god. It should be eighty four angula (finger's breadth) long. The face should be of twelve angulas measure. Of this one third would be accounted for by the chin of the icon. The rest would be taken up by the nose and the forehead of the image. The eyes should be of two angulas, half of it should go to form the retina. The pupil must be one-third the size of the retina. The total measure of the face should be thirty two angulas. The length of the nose and that of the neck should be identical. The arms and forearms, the legs and thighs should be of even measure. The feet should be six angulas long and four angulas broad. The nails and toes should be comparatively smaller.

The eyes must be large, the lips red and the face like a blooming lotus. The shoulders, the chest, the thighs, the eyebrows, the forehead, the nose and the cheeks should be prominent and uplifted.[1]

The trees with only two branches, the trees having the decadent wood—which have dried due to age, the trees having a very brittle wood, the trees that exude honey, oil or red fluid (blood-like) should be scrupulously avoided for making a wooden icon.

When the icon has been made it should be washed in Gangajal before adorning it with jewels, ear-rings, garlands, crown and a yagyopaveeta. A small garland made of the lotus flowers or a golden necklace should be held in the hands of the icon.

---

1. Although the regional preferences determine the aesthetics of the features, what is described here forms the preference of the images made in Central and North India.

All these precautions must be taken because if the image is not proportional or broken in any way, instead of bestowing favour, it might invoke the wrath of the gods.

The Purana also lists the consequence of having a badly formed image. If any part of the image is larger than its prescribed dimension, the danger may threaten the entire kingdom (or region). In case the organs of the image are shorter than prescribed the region (or the kingdom) may be ravaged by diseases or epidemic. A larger belly threatens hunger and famine afflicting the people but if the belly is too small it forebodes widespread poverty. Should a belly (or the image) be cracked it indicates an impending war.

Should the image be slanting towards right the people of the region may have their life-span reduced. On the other hand its slant toward left signifies marital squabbles among the people of the region. Should the eyes be slanting upwards the builder of the image may go blind. Their downward slant threatens much financial and physical difficulties to the people.

It is obvious that an image or icon of any god must be made with due precaution and care.

4

The Past, Present And Future Dynasties

The final chapter of the Bhavishya Purana deals with future which distinguishes this Purana from other Puranas. It is owing to its so copiously referring about future that it earned its name 'Bhavishya Purana'. This part deals with future happenings. It covers such a vast span of 'ndian history—right from the accession of Manu to the throne to advent of the British in India and the rule of Queen Victavati (Victoria) that it made the scholars date its compilation somewhere in the end of the 18th century AD. Although it describes the events in the future tense, it is eminently clear that most of them are coeval with its compilation. Apart from mentioning the names of the kings of the Solar and Lunar dynasties, it also refers about the Rajputa kings of the Middle Ages like Prithvi Raj Chauhan and Jai Chanda but even mention about the 'Mlechcha rule' spearheaded by Babur, Humayun, Sher Shah, Akbar. It also mentions about Shivaji, Mahadaji Scindia (Sindhia) and indirectly refers about the English words like 'Sunday', 'February' and 'sixty'. It even describes in future tense the establishment of the British Rule. But it refers all these events in a swipe as if they are part of the mighty history current of time in Indian peninsula.

The Advent of Manu and the Kali Age and Its Dynasties

Before referring about the Kali Age, it starts its Pratisarga Parva the rules of Manu Vaivasvata, the subsequent generation during the Treta and Dwapar Ages.

Solar Dynasty

The Sootaji starts the narration from the advent of Vaivasvata Manu who reigned during the last half of Brahma's Age. He was followed by Ikshvaaku who ruled from Ayodhya, on the banks of Saraju for 3600 years. But his son Vikukshi could rule for only 100 years. His son Ripunjaya could rule even less. In fact the subsequent rulers of this dyanasty, which continued this way—Anenaas, Prithu, Vimbagashva, Ardranaam, Bhadrashcha, Yuvanashcha, Shravastha (who established the famous city of Sravasthi), Vrihadashva, Kuvalayashva—could not rule for more than a hundred years. But Kuvalayashva's son Nikumbhaka had ruled for more than a 1000 years. His son was Sankatashva. Other famous rulers of this dynasty were Prasenjit and Tadra Varnashva whose son was renowned Mandhata.

Mandhata's son was Purukutsa who could not rule for a hundred years. His son Trishadashva was renowned for yoking as many as 30 horses in his chariot. Trishadashva's son was Anaranya who had ruled for twenty eight years only.

This period figures in the second part of the Satya Yuga. Then this dynasty had an illustrious ruler called Prishadashva who had ruled for 6000 years. The dynasty then continued the following manner: Prishadashva → Hariashva → Vasuma → Tatvidhanva → Tridhanva → Triyaranya who ruled for more than 1000 years. He was followed by his son, Trishanku[1]. His rule was deceitfully snatched. His son was the famous veridicious king Harishchandra whose confrontation with Vishwamitra is a well known story.

Harishchandra's son was Rohitashva and then the lineage progressed this way: Rohitashva → Chanchabhoopa → Tadruka → Sagar.

Sagar is believed to have ruled in the third phase of the Satya Yuga. He was a great devotee of Lord Shiv. It was his sons who disturbed Kapil Muni's penance to face instant incineration by the sage's fiery gaze. His son was Anshuman whose son was Dilip. It was the son of King Dilip, Bhagiratha, who endeavoured hard to bring the Ganga on the mortal plains to make his grand uncle's soul's redemption. Bhagiratha's son was Shrutasena who ruled

---

1. Read in detail about this story in the Devi Bhagwata Purana of the same series. From the king's name the term 'Trishanku' has been taken which means held in abeyance i.e. neither in the sky nor on the earth.

for less than 100 years. His son was Ambareesha, the famous devotee of Lord Vishnu.

Ambareesha's son was Sindhudweepa. Then the lineage continued the following way: Sindhudweepa → Ayutashva → Rituparna → Kalyana → Pada → Sudasa → Adashamaka → Hariverma → Dashratha → Vishwasaba. During Vishwasaba's rule anarchy had reigned as much as to cause the minor Pralaya. The king had to stay for ten years in the caves of the Himalaya with his priest, chosen traders and ministers. After 10 years when the earth became solid and dry particularly in this part of the world, the king very devotedly prayed to Goddess Mahamaya who made every thing normal. Since then the tradition started of praying to the Goddess Mahamaya immediately after rains. After ruling for ten millennia the king expired. He was followed by Raja Dilip who got a son, blessed by a cow called Nandini, Raghu. It was after his name that this branch of the solar dynasty came too be called Raghuvansha. Raghu had a brilliant son named Aja. Aja was also a very powerful king who managed to subdue all the kings of the earth. During his rule, Ayodhya became the most important city of the world. His son was Dashrath, the famous ruler of Ayodhya who had four illustrious sons called Ram, Bharat, Lakshmana and Shatrughna.

Lord Hari (Vishnu) had incarnated himself in the form of Raja Ram who ruled for 11,000 years. Lord Ram was succeeded by his son Kush who also ruled for 10,000 years. Subsequently in this dynasty the other important ruler was Kuru and then the lineage continued in the following way: Kuru → Dalapaal → Chhadmakari → Uktha → Vajarabhi → Shaga → Vyurthanabhi → Vishwapaal → Swarnanabhi → Pushpasen → Dhruva → Upavarma → Sheeghraganta → Marupaal → Susandha who ruled upto the second phase of the Treta Yuga. Then the lineage progressed in the following way: Susandhi → Bhamarbha → Mahaashva → Vrihadbaal → Vriha daishan → Murukshepa → Vatsavaal → Vatsavyooha → Jyoma → Suprateeka → Sunakshatra → Keshinara → Autarikaha → Survanaga → Vrihadraja → Dharmaraja → Kritanjaya → Sanjaya → Shakyavardhana → Krodhadaan → Tulavikram → Prasenjit → Shoodraka → Suratha. All of these kings had ruled well to continue the hold of Ayodhya kingdom over the world. In all, this way, as many as 65 rulers had ruled in the Raghu's branch of the solar dynasty.

Lunar Dynasty

According to Bhavishya Purana this dynasty began to rule from the third phase of the Treta Yuga. Indra had established Chandrama (Moon) on the earth who was a great devotee of Lord Vishnu and Shiv. Chandrama (or Chandra) eloped with the wife of Vrihaspati, called Tara, and produced a son from this union whose name was Budha[1] (Mercury). The lunar dynasty thus began the following way: Chandra → Budha → Merudeva → Puroorava, Aayu and Nahusha. Among these the most notable was Nahusha who could become as much powerful as to snatch the throne of the divine chief Indra. But the curse from the great sage Durvasa made him a python. His son Jayati had five sons out of which three turned Mlechcha. But his two remaining sons made the lineage continue the following way (this line started from Yadu). Yadu → Koshtha → Vrijonhana → Swahaarchana → Chitrarath → Arvinda → Shrava → Taamas → Ushana → Sheetanshuka → Kamalanshu → Paravata → Jaamaga → Vidharbha → Krata Kuntibhoja.

The other son was Puru who continued the lineage in the following manner: Puru → Vrashaparvana → Mayavidhya → Janmejaya → Prachinvan → Nabhasya → Bhavada → Sudyumna → Bahugara → Sayati → Dhanayati → Eindrashiva → Rantnara → Sutapa → Samvarana. Samvarana had performed a rigorous penance in the Himalayana cave to please Lord Surya who granted him a daughter called Tapti. Delighted, he repaired to the realm of the sun. Meanwhile the Bharata-Khanda of the Jambudweepa faced a mini-pralaya for two years. Thereafter the strong winds dried its land and Sage Agastya made the earth solid with green vegetation.

But this time the Age Dwapar had started. The Sootaji

---

1. This astrological-cum-mythological event has been vividly described in the Shiv Purana of our same series of the Puranas. The desirous readers may get details from that book.

told that on the 13th lunar day of the month of Bhadrapada, Raja Samvarana returned to the earth to rule over it for a period of 10,000 years. From Samavarana the lineage resumed the following manner: Samavarana → Archanga → Suryajaapi → Suryayagya → Aathithyavardhana → Dwaadashatma → Diwakara → Prabhakara → Bhasvadaatma → Vivaswaja → Haridashwarchana → Vaikartana. All of them ruled like their fathers for less than a hundred years. From Vaikartana's son Arkeshtimana this branch continued upto Yagyaka. In this family there appeared a very great scholar called Vairochana who eventually became the ruler of this branch. Then the lineage resumed the following way: Vairochana → Vedapravardhana → Savitra → Dhanapal → Anandavardhana → Dharmapal who was a great devotee of Lord Supreme. His son's name was Brahmeshthivardhana → Parameshthi → Hairanyavardhana → Dhatriyaji → Dhartriprapoojaka → Drohinakratu → Pratansa. Pratansa's son was Paratansa in whose seventh generation had appeared Dushyanta who married Shakuntala (the daughter of Sage Vishwamitra and Apsara Menaka). It was Dushyanta's son Bharat who was the most illustrious king of this dynasty. It is after his name that Jambudweepa's this part came to be called Bharatavarsha. Blessed by Goddess Mahamaya he had ruled for 36000 years. Bharat's son was Mahabali Pratapendra who ruled over India for 10,000 years. Then this lineage continued the following manner: Pratapendra → Mandaleeka → Vijayendra → Dhanurdweepa → Hasti.

It was Hasti whose son was fabled Eiravata elephant's son Gaja. Hasti established the famous city Hastinapur (of Mahabharat fame). Hasti's branch had a scion called Ajaameedha who had an illustrious son called Kuru. He was so powerful that owing to a boon he received from Indra, he had gone to heaven with his mortal body intact.

During this very age in a branch of this dynasty had emerged a Saatvata family whose one scion, Vrishni, was very powerful. Blessed by Lord Narayana he ruled for 5,000 years. Then his lineage progressed the following way: Vrishni → Nrivritti → Dashari → Vyayuna → Jeemuta → Vikrata → Bheemaratha → Navarath → Dashrath →

Shakuni → Kushumbh → Devarath → Devakshetra → Madhu → Navarath → Kuruvatsa → Anurath → Puruhotra → Vichitranga → Saatvatavan → Yajamana → Vidurath → Surabhakta → Tatikshetra → Swyaayambhuva → Surapala. He got a son from an Apsara, Sukeshi. His name was Kuru who established the famous place Kurukshetra. Kuru had ruled for 12,000 years.

His son's name was Jahnu and then the lineage continued this way: → Suratha, → Vidurath → Sarva-Bhaum → Jayasena → Arnava → Ayutayu → Akrodhana → Riksha → Bheemsena → Dilip → Prateepa → Shaantanu → Vichitraveerya. Vichitraveerya had two sons: Dhritarashtra and Pandu. Since Dhritarashtra was born blind, Pandu became the ruler. But Pandu soon expired and Dhritarashtra became the regent. Under his regency his son Duryodhana had ruled for sixty years. Then Yudhishthir, the eldest Pandava, ascended to the throne and he ruled for 50 years. After the Pandavas retired to the Himalayas, Arjuna's grandson Pareekshita ascended to the throne. His son was Janmejaya who was a very powerful ruler. In order to avenge his father's untimely demise he threatened to exterminate the entire race of the serpents. His son's name was Shataneeka who ruled very ably. Then the lineage progressed the following manner: Shataneeka → Yagyadutta → Nishchakra → Tadushtapal → Chitrarath → Dhritiman → Sushena → Suneetha → Makhpaal → Nachakshu → Sukhavata → Pariplava → Munash → Kripanchaya → Mridu → Tigujyoti → Vribadratha → Vasudana → Shataneeka → Udyaan → Ahira → Nimitra → Deemaka → Kshemaka.

It was Kshemaka who killed all the Mlechcha and recaptured his rule following Narada's advice. Kshemaka's son was Pradyota whose son was Vedavana who ruled for two thousand years.

In the sub-branch of this dynasty, Vrishni, there appeared Lord Krishna under whose guidance all rulers of Bharatavarsha had ruled. Lord Krishna's mortal age was 135 years. The age of Dwapar had ended with Lord Krishna's quitting his mortal coil.

Then the Sootaji recounted the dynasties of the Kali Age.

The Dynasties of the Kali Yuga (Age)

Curiously enough, the Bhavishya Purana catalogues the dynasties of the Kali Age which had yet to happen. Although this material may also be found in other Puranas, like the Matsya Purana and Vayu Purana, all Puranas clearly trace the origin of this kind of material to the Bhavishya Purana only. The Bhavishya Purana asserts that the exit of Lord Krishna from this earth and the dawn of the Kali Age took place simultaneously.

[As is well known, a Yug or Age is a very big unit. Their cycle is made of four Ages viz Satya (Krita), Treta, Dwapar and Kali Yugas. Accordingly the general moral standard will decline with the worst human features dominating the Kali Age].

The Bhavishya Purana says that the Kali Age will be an evil era. It will bring an invasion from the west of Yavanas. [The Yavanas are identified with the Greeks]. In this age upstart races, declining as soon as they rise, will succeed each other in ruling the earth. But this Age will see the mingling of the Aryan and the Mlechcha races. Unrighteous kings will freely kill each other.

This Purana declares that it will deal with the future—the future that follows the Mahabharat War. Given below are the dynasties that will exist in this Kali Age:

[In fact the dynasties that reigned in North India in the period following the Mahabharat War were incorporated in couplets that were composed and set to tune. These couplets were sung by bards and minstrels in the languages called Prakrata, Magadhi and Pali. The compiler of the Bhavishya Purana apparently appropriated these couplets, converted them into Sanskrit and altered them to the form of prophecies believed to have been made by the great sage Vedavyasa. This process continued not only in the initial period (between 3rd & 4th AD) but also upto the advent of the British Rule in India. This way the text of this Purana was kept well updated till almost the end of the 18th century AD.]

The Bhavisya Purana gives the following dynasties that would reign in the Kali Age:

(i) The Paurava

As we have listed the earlier rulers of the lunar dynasty, we shall start with Janmejaya, the son of Pareekshita of the Mahabharat fame.

Janmejaya's son was Shatanika, whose son was chivalrous Ashwamedhadutta. His son was Adhisimhakrishna who reigns now in great fame. [This assertion clearly suggests that the text was compiled during Adhisimhakrishna's rule.]

Adhisimhakrishna's son will be Nichakshu. [It is during his reign that Hastinapur was flooded and carried away by the Ganga. It was during this period that Nichakshu had shifted his capital to Kaushambi, near modern Allahabad]. He will have eight sons of great might and valour. His eldest son will be Ushna who will be followed by Chitrarath. He will be replaced by his son Shuchidratha whose son Vrishnimat will rule them. His son Sushena will be a righteous king. Then the lineage will continue the following way: Sushena → Sumitha → Rucha → Nrichakshus → Sukhibala → Pariplava → Sunaya → Medhavin → Nripanjaya → Durva → Tigataman → Brihadratha → Vasudana → Shatanik → Udayana. Udayana will be a famous king as well as the lute player. He will be followed by Vahinara whose son will be Dandapani. After Dandapani will rule Niramitra and this lineage will end with Kshemaka.

There will be 25 kings in this race of Puru. This Paurava dynasty will reach its end in the Kali Age with Kshemaka. Thus this race which started with Arjuna, the third Pandava, will hold sway over the Aryavarta for about 500 years.

(ii) **The lineage of the Ikshvakus**: This is an illustrious branch of the solar dynasty whose details before the advent of the Kali Yug have already been given. At the beginning of Kali Yuga Brihadbala was ruling. His heir was the warrior king Brihatshaya. He was followed by Urukshaya → Vatsavyooha → Prativyom.

Prativyom's son was Diwakara who now rules in the city of Ayodhya. [The use of the present there indicates that this part of the Bhavishya Purana was composed during the rule of Diwakara].

Diwakara's successor will be the famous Sahadeva whose heir would be noble-natured Brihadashva. Then the lineage will continue the following manner: Brihadashva → Bhanuratha → Pratitashva → Supratika → Merudeva → Sunakshatra → Kinnarashva, the victorious → Antariksha → Suparna → Amitarajit → Brihadbhrija → Dharmin → Kritanjaya → Rananjaya → Sanjaya, the warrior king → Shakya → Shuddhodhana

[Shuddhodhana is that famous king who was father of Siddhartha (Gautam), the Buddha who started the faith of Buddhism.]

Shuddhodhana → Siddhartha (Gautam, the enlightened one. Since he abdicated the throne his son Rahula was installed as the king. Then the lineage resumed this way: Rahula → Prasenjit → Kshudvaka → Kulaka → Suratha → Sumitra who shall be the last king of this sub-branch of the solar dynasty. All these kings will bring glory to the family owing to their erudition and able administration. This race will terminate with Sumitra.

[Whether they were the predictions made by the Bhavishya Purana or the mere interpolation from other sources, most of these details stand corroborated by actual historical records.]

(iii) **Brihadrathas**: This was the race started by the ruler of the Magadha Kshetra. At the fag end of the Dwapar Age, Sahadeva, the son of the tyrant ruler Jarasandha, was ruling. Sahadeva was slain in the Kurukshetra (Mahabharat) war. His successor was Somadhi who ruled from his capital in Girivraja for 58 years. In this line Shushmutashrava was the king for 64 years. Ayutayu who succeeded him was the ruler for 26 years. His successor Niramitra enjoyed the earth for 40 years before ascending to heaven. He was followed by Sukshatara who ruled for 56 years. His successor was Brihatkarman who reigned for 23 years. Now Senajit is ruling who shall rule for 23 years. Then the lineage will continue the following manner (Given in the bracket are the number of years each ruler of this dynasty will rule for):

Shatrunjaya (40) → Vibhu (28) → Shuchi (58) → Suvrata (64) → Sunetra (35) → Nivritti (58) → Trinetra (28) → Dridhasena (48) → Mahinetra (33) → Suchala (32) → Sunetra (40) → Satyajit (83) → Vishvajet (25) → Ripunjaya (50). These 16 kings will be known in the future as Brihadvathas. The Purana predicts that their kingdom will last for 723 years. In all there will be comparatively 32 insignificant rulers and they will rule for a full 1000 years.

(iv) **The Pradyotas**: After the Brihadrathas exit from the scene (which shall be caused by their commander, Pulika, revolting and coming to the saddle), Pradyota, the son of Pulika, will be the king. Pradyota will be able to subdue all the kings of the region and he would act like an overlord to rule for 23 years. He will be followed by Palaaka who shall rule for 24 years. He will be succeeded by Vishkhyarupa who will rule for 50 years. Then will rule Ajaka for 21 years and he will be succeeded by Nandavihardana for 20 years. Thus the Pradyota dynasty will rule for nearly 150 years.

(v) **The Dynasty of Shishunagas**: Displacing the Pradyota, Shishunaga will ascend to the throne. He would make Girivraja his capital city. His son will rule from Kashi. Shishunaga will rule for 40 years and his son Kakavarna for 36 years. After Kakavarna Kshemadharman will be the king for the next 20 years and he will be followed by Khastrojas who shall rule for 40 years. He will be succeeded by the famous king Bimbasara who shall rule for 28 years. His son [the renowned king], Ajatashatru, will rule for 25 years. Then the Shishunaga dynasty will progress this way: Ajatashatru → Darshaka → Udayin (33). Udayin will again shift his capital to Kusumpura, on the southern bank of the river Ganga, in the fourth year of his reign. He will be succeeded by Nandivardhana (40 yrs) and Mahanandin (43 yrs). Thus there will rule 10 Shishunaga kings and their dynastic hold shall continue for 163 years.

Some contemporaneous dynasties will be Panchalas, Haihayas, Kalingas, Ashmakas, Maithalas, Shaurasenas and Vitihotras[1].

(vi) **The Nandas**: [The last Shishunag] King Mahanandin (or Mahananda) will have a son from a Shoodra woman. He will be called Mahapadma Nanda and he will try to exterminate all the Kshatriya Kings. All the kings thereafter will be of Shoodra origin. This powerful king, Mahapadma Nanda, will bring the entire earth under his rule and will

---

1. Owing to paucity of space only prominent dynasties are being referred to here. Other less renowned are being alluded to in a passing reference.

reign for 88 years. He will have 8 sons, of whom Sukalpa will be the eldest. [His name, according to other sources, will be Nanda]. His three sons will succeed Mahapadma Nanda and shall rule for 12 years. Then a Brahmin named Kautilya (Chanakya) will uproot the Nandas. After the Nandas have ruled for 100 years, the Mauryas will assume the authority and shall rule the earth.

(vii) **The Mauryas**: Having caused the fall of the Nanda dynasty, Kautilya will appoint Chandragupta as the king of Magadha. He will rule for 24 years, followed by Bindusar who shall rule for 25 years. He will be succeeded by Ashoka who will rule for 36 years. Ashoka's son Kunala will reign for 8 years. He will be succeeded by his son Bandhupalita who shall rule for 8 years. Then his heir Indrapalita will rule for 10 years. He will be succeeded by Devavarmana who will be the king for 7 years. Then his son Shatadhanu will rule for 7 years. Thus the 9 Mauryas will rule the earth for a total of 137 years. They will be replaced by Pushyamitra who shall establish the rule of his Shunga Dynasty.

(viii) **The Shungas**: Pushyamitra, the general of the Brihadrathas, will eliminate his king and establish a new dynasty, called the Shungas. Pushyamitra will rule for 36 years. His son Agnimitra will rule for 8 years and then the lineage will progress in the following way: Vasujyeshtha (7 yrs) → Vasumitra (10 yrs) → Andhraka (2 yrs) → Pulindaka (3 yrs) → Ghosa (3 yrs). Then another general of the same family, Vajramitra, will be the king for 9 years. He will be replaced by his son, Bhagawata, who shall rule for 32 years. The last ruler of this dynasty will be Devabhumi. Thus ten Shunga kings will rule the earth—combinedly—for 112 years. Then the ruler of the earth shall be the Kanvas.

(ix) **The Kanvas**: This dynasty is also called Kanvayana. Its first ruler will be Vasudeva who would be the minister of the displaced Shunga King Devabhumi. He shall establish the rule of his **Kanvayana** dynasty. Vasudeva will rule for 14 years and then he will be succeeded by his son Narayana who will reign for 12 years. His successor will be his son Susharmana who shall rule for 10 years. The Kanvayana will be the Bramin rulers. They will rule for 45 years. They shall be righteous and fair kings and they would be displaced by the Andhras.

(x) **The Andhras**: The Andhras will be of the tribal rulers. The Andhra Simuka and his fellow tribesmen will be the servants of the Kanva King Susharmana. But the Andhras will eventually remove the Karva King Susharmana to set up their own dynasty on the throne of authority.

After Simuka having ruled for 23 years, his younger brother, Krishna, will rule for 10 years. He will be followed by his younger brother, Shri Shatakarni, who shall rule for 18 years. Then the dynastic rule will progress the following way: Purnotsanga (18 years) → Skandastambhi (18 yrs) → Shatakarni (56 yrs) → (his son) Lambodara (18 years) → Apilaka (12 years) → Meghasvati (18 years) → Svati (18 yrs). The last ruler of this dynasty will be Skandavati who shall rule for only 7 years.

Then another branch of this dynasty, spearheaded by Swatikarna, will reign for 3 years. The name of this king will be Mrigendra. He will be replaced by Kuntala Swatikarna who shall rule for 8 years. Then the dynasty shall progress this way: Kuntala → Pulomavi (36 yrs) → Arishthakarna (25 yrs) → Hala (5 yrs) → Mantalaka (5 years) → Purikshena (21 yrs) → Sundara Shatakarni (6 months) → Shivasvati (28 yrs) → Gantamputra (21 yrs) → Puloma (28 yrs) → Shivashri Puloma (7 yrs) → Shivaskandha Shatakarni (3 yrs) → Vijaya (6 yrs) → Chandashri Shatakarni (10 yrs). The last ruler of this dynasty shall be Pulomavi who will reign for 7 years.

Thus in all there will be thirty kings of this dynasty who shall rule the earth for 460 years.

(xi) **Vidisha Dynasties**: Vidisha, being a great power centre and a renowned city of Central India (near modern Indore), also had many able rulers who held their sway in this part of the world.

According to the Bhavishya Purana this centre will be established by Bhogin, the son of the Naga king, Shesha[1].

---

1. Generally the Naag tribes referred to in this and other Puranas give the impression as if they were the tribes of the scrpents. But this is not the truth. In fact the Naag tribes mean those primitive or aboriginal tribes of the region whose totem was a Naag or a serpent. They worshipped the Naag as a deity only, Shesha being their primordial deity, often reffered to as the thousand-headed serpent Shesha Naag.

He will conquer the cities of his enemies and will bring much glory to this Naag tribe. He will be replaced by Sadachandra. Chandransha shall be the third king of this dynasty. He will be succeeded by Dhanadharmana who shall be displaced by Vangara. Vangara will be succeeded by Bhootinanda.

At the termination of the Shungas' dynasty, Shishunandi will reign. His younger brother will be Nandiyasha and three more kings will reign after him. Nandiyasha's grandson (daughter's son will be Shishuka and he will rule in Purika (modern Puri).

Vindhyashati's valiant son will be Pravira and he will rule over the city of Kanchanaka for 60 years. He will also conduct many sacrifices and his four sons will establish separate kingdoms.

(xii) Local And Other Dynasties (3rd Century A.D.):

After listing the prominent dynasties separately the Bhavishya Purana records the future existence of many other dynasties.

When the kingdom of the Andhras has come to an end, there will be kings belonging to the lineage of their servants. There will be seven Shriparvatiya Andhras, 10 Abhira kings, 7 Gardabhins and 18 Shakas. There will also be 8 Yavanas, 14 Tusharas, 13 Murundas and 11 Maunas. The Shriparvatiya Andhras will last for 52 years, the 10 Abhira kings for 67 years, the 7 Gardabhins for 72 years, 18 Shakas for 183 years, 8 Yavanas for 87 years. The Purana claims that earth shall be ruled by Tusharas for 7000 years. The 13 Murundas, along with lowly Mlechchas, will enjoy the earth for 200 years. The 11 Maunas will enjoy it for 103 years. When they are finally overthrown by time, there will be the Kilakila kings. After the term of the Kilakilas is over, King Vindhyashakti will rule strongly for as many as 96 years.

When the family of the Vindhyakas has passed away, there will be 3 Vahlika kings. Supratika and Nabhir will enjoy the rule of the earth for 30 years. Shakyamana shall be Mahishis' king. In Mekala, 7 kings will reign for 70 years. In Koshala there will be 9 very powerful and wise kings, renowned as the Meghas. All the rulers of Nishadha, born in the family of Nala, will be valiant and very powerful and shall exist till this Manuvantar ends.

Among the valiant Maghadhas, the most chivalrous king shall be Vishvasphani. Overthrowing all Kshatriya kings, he will make kings from classes other than the Kshatriya class—Kaivartas, Panchakas, Pulindas and the Brahmanas. In various countries they shall be established as the rulers. Vishvasphani will be as powerful in battle as Vishnu is reputed to be. Having propitiated the gods through his great deeds, be will retire to the bank of the holy Ganga to end his life. Following his death he shall stay in Indra's realm for many years.

The Champavati city shall be ruled by 7 Naga kings. Then they would have Mathura as their capital.

With the advent of the Gupta dynasty, all the territories along the banks of Ganga viz Prayag, Saketa and Magadha shall fall under their control. Kings born from Manidhanya will enjoy the territories of the Naishadhas, Yadukas, Shaishitas and Kalatakoyas. The Devarakshita will enjoy the rule over the Koshala, Andhras, Paundras, Tamralptas and the charming city of Champa.

In the Kalinga region Guha will be the king while Mahishas and the inhabitants of the Mahendra mountains shall rule the hilly terrain. The Shoodras and outcastes shall rule over Sourashtras, Avantyas, Abhiras, Arbudas and Malava. The rivers Sindhu (Indus), Chandrabhaga (Chenab) and Kounti shall be ruled by such destitute people. All these kings will be lacking in grace. They shall be untruthful and of unrighteous conduct.

The Rationale Behind the Mention of These Dynasties in the Bhavishya Purana

Apparently these references may seem to be filling the pages of the Purana without any relevance. However, it is not the case. They have a wide ranging significance for they help in pinpointing any specific occurrence of a historic event. Counting backwards on the basis of the generations passed we can get the actual date of any famous historical event. Take, for example, the date of ascertaining the actual period of occurrence of the Mahabharat.

As a matter of fact, there are three ways of doing it, with one of them being going by the genealogies given in the Purana. The others are using the astronomical data on the position of the Nakshatras mentioned in the Mahabharata. But, probably because of later interpolation which were freely introduced, such information tends to be mutually inconsistent and yields quite divergent dates like 3140 BC, 3137 BC, 1400 BC, 1197 BC and 1151 BC etc. The second approach is to date the Kurukshetra War on the basis of the astronomical traditions of famous astronomers like Aryabhatta, and Varahamihira. According to the Aryabhatta tradition, the Kali Age began in the year 3102 BC. So, by this date the Mahabharat War should have taken place around the year 3138 BC. But the Varahamihira tradition places the war in 2449 BC. However, the scholars won't accept both of the traditions as a war consuming as many as 36,36,600[1] men (or nearly 40,00,000 men) couldn't have taken place then.

This confusion makes only the genealogical charts given in the Bhavishya Purana as the only relevant means to determine the date of the Mahabharata. From accounts left by the Greek historian Megasthenes, one can match it with the period when the Maurya dynasty's Chandragupta existed. Taking that period as the reckoning factor, with the help of the genealogical accounts given in this Purana—taking 20 years for one generation—one can reasonably come close to ascertaining the war's occurrence. Going through the process the scholars believe that the war should have taken place about 5000 years ago. Hence the relevance of the dynasties mentioned in the various Puranas—particularly the Bhavishya Purana which is believed to be comprising the most reliable historical account.

Apart from these calculations which are made by the records mentioned in the Bhavishya Purana, there are also such details in it as are prevalent as customs in the society of the devouts. One of them is the recital of 'Shree Satyanarain Katha'. The devout have this recital made by

---

1. The total consumption was 18 Akshohinis. Each Akshohini is made up of 21,870 chariots, 21,870 elephants, 65,610 horses and 1,09,350 infantry men. If one allows one charioteer per chariot, one driver per elephant and one rider per horse, this makes 2,18,700 men per Akshohini which for 18 Akshohinis become 39,36,600 men.

the learned priest which is made as a means of thanksgiving on some desired endeavour's successful completion or it is also done in anticipation of (and prayer for) the successful completion of the long cherished project. The Satyanarain Katha also forms the part of this Bhavishya Purana which is given ahead in details.

5

The Satyanarain Katha[1] And Other Tales

[This Katha's recital is a ceremonious event. The priest and listeners should be duly invited at the given time and place and following its completion within scheduled time, the 'Prasadam' is also distributed among them.]

The Bhavishya Purana says that Satyanarain Katha is bliss-giving and distress-removing for all. Those who have some specific desire or those who want to thank God for granting one the completion of the desired objective have this Katha ceremoniously recited. As such there is no 'katha' but it tells the consequences of one's going back upon one's word.

Before starting this Katha the following Mantra should be chanted by the person (or by his priest on his behalf) for 108 times. The Mantra is:

"*Om Namo Bhagwate Nitya Satya Sevaya Dheemahi.*"
While chanting this mantra the mind should be concentrated on Lord Narain (Vishnu) and after having chanted the mantra the host should say: "*Chatuh Padaartha Gaatre Cha Namastubhyam Namo Namah*" and offer flowers before the idol of Lord Narain or His representative, the Shaligram.

The origin of this custom was started by the experience of a Brahmin who was distressed with difficulties. He had happened to hear in a recitation that he who heard the Satyanarain Katha's glories with rapt attenption would have all his troubles eliminated. So he decided that on the following day if he got enough money, he would devote it to the worship and obeisance of Lord Satyanarain. As good luck would have it, he really got much more money than

---

1. The essence of this Katha is that Truth (Satya) should be taken as adorable as God and one should never go back on one's word.

he had ever expected. Immediately he came home and told his wife about this exhilarating experience. She immediately advised her husband to hold this Katha ceremony with great fanfare. In that recital they invited all their friends and relatives. After the 'Katha' he told them how he came about holding this Katha ceremony. All were very much impressed and they all decided to follow suit in case of distress. This is how this custom commenced.

Continuing the narration the Sootaji told that similar had been the experience of a Bheel. Sudama, the friend of Lord Krishna, had his tale of sudden prosperity known to all.

Then he told the tale of Raja Chandrachooda who had fallen on evil days and after his holding the ceremony of Satyanarain Katha, he was relieved of his distress.

Similar was the tale of Lilavati. His father was a sea trader and once he was coming back home on a ship, he found on the shore a gathering of people devoted to worship. Upon inquiry he learnt that they all were listening to the Katha of Satyanarain. He also promised to hold such a recital provided he reached well home. Till that time he had no issue. Reaching home safe he held the katha. With the result, he also got a daughter named Lilavati. As she came of age he got her married to a young trader who was his business partner. Now the trader was passing life very happily but he had forgotten to hold the Katha of Satyanarain after his daughter's marriage.

One day while he was returning from his long voyage with his boat full of costly gems and gold, the boat was held by the king of the shore and both the father-in-law and the son-in-law were put in the jail. Now, this was a bolt from the blue. They were held guilty of the theft that they had never committed. While languishing in the jail, the father-in-law realised that he had not kept his word of holding the ceremony of the Satyanarain Katha recital following the birth of his daughter. But since they could attend the Katha recital held at the shore, they were eventually released from the jail and they happily reached their home. As soon as they reached there they held the Katha ceremony to the great delight of their family. Ever since then the Brahmin family lived happily. This way, according to the Purana, holding the Katha ensures everybody's welfare.

Other Tales of Historical Significance

As we have already hinted, the Bhavishya Purana contains many 'future tales'. Many of them are of great historical significance. A few of them are given below:

(i) Prithvi Raj Chauhan and Jai Chanda

Narrating the happenings that occurred in the Jambudweepa, Sootaji recounted the following story:

In the medieval times, there was a king of Indraprastha. His name was Anangapal. He was very powerful and he had almost the entire central part of India under his command. But he had no male issue. When he performed the Yagya for getting a male issue, instead of a son he got two daughters. Their names were Chandrakanta and Keertimalini. When they came of age he got them married to the kings of Kanyakubja and Ajmer respectively. The name of the king of Ajmer was Someshwara. At this time only, there was a Brahmin named Jaisharma. When he saw the king Anangapal donating out his affluence in his daughters' marriage, in order to get them he started to observe great penance in the Himalayas. There he quitted his mortal coil and took his next birth as the son of Chandrakanta. Later on he became famous as Jai Chanda. Meanwhile Keertimalini had three sons and the middle one was named Prithvi Raj Chauhan. He was partially adopted by Raja Anangapal and became the ruler of Indraprastha (Delhi) following Anangapal's death. Prithvi Raj was a robust person with a grand personality. He was very brave and chivalrous and soon became the overlord of the entire region around Delhi.

Meanwhile, Jai Chanda—another grandson of Anangapal from his daughter's side—continued to nurse an ill-will against Prithvi Raj for having usurped his maternal grandfather's (Anangapal's) entire kingdom. He wrote a letter to Prithvi Raj demanding half of the kingdom of Raja Anangapal as his due share. He also warned that should this demand be not met, it would result into a fierce confrontation. But Prithvi Raj pompously replied that in order to neutralise the rogues of the lunar dynasty, he had already collected an army of twenty lakh soldiers. He also wrote that, on the contrary, since he was the overlord of entire India, it was incumbent upon Jai Chanda to pay him the tax.

When this kind of scathing letters continued to be exchanged, both the kings developed severe animosity between them. Meanwhile, the daughter of Jai Chanda, Sanyogita, became nubile. She was a beautiful girl. She had also heard about Prithvi Raj. Also, she had known about Prithvi Raj's bravery and robustness. So, when her Swayamvara was announced, Prithvi Raj made his trusted sleuth, Priya Bhatt, arrange for Sanyogita's elopement by him.

In the Swayamvara, in order to insult the Delhi ruler, Prithvi Raj, Jai Chanda kept a statue of Prithvi Raj at the very gate of that huge assembly. But with the help of his pet sleuth, Priya Bhatt, Prithvi Raj not only reached the venue of the Swayamvara secretly but also managed to hide himself behind his own statue. And as Sanyogita, who had heard about Prithvi Raj reaching the place, neglected all the invited princes and kings and put the garland around the neck of the statue totally defying his father's wishes. Prithvi Raj quickly came out from the hiding place and carrying Sanyogita on his hands, jumped on his ready horse and sped away with her. This created a furore in Kanyakubja and Jai Chanda asked his army to follow and capture Prithvi Raj. But Prithvi Raj had also made his army ready and a fierce battle ensued between his forces and the forces of Jai Chanda. The battle lasted for six days but eventually Prithvi Raj managed to reach Delhi with Samyogita. Jai Chanda was defeated and this event made Prithvi Raj the effective overlord of entire India to the great chagrin of Jai Chanda. [It was he who eventually, out of sheer jealousy, invited the Mlechcha ruler, Shahabuddin Gauri, to have Prithvi Raj defeated. This led to the establishment of the Mlechcha raj in India].

[Apart from this story of Prithvi Raj, the Bhavishya Purana also recounts many stories of the earlier Medieval India including that of the famous Alha (Ahlaada) and Malakhaan (called Balakhana) in a casual way. These stories are too clumsily mentioned to deserve their reference here as apparently they form the part of the interpolations added subsequently to this Purana. In fact it mentions about many stories of the Medieval India in a most haphazard manner. Prominent ones are related to birth of Ramanujacharya, Shankaracharya, Varahamihira, even that of Timirlung (Taimur-Lung), Akbar and Aurangzeb, Vikram and Vaitala etc. They are not being covered here for the simple reason as they are too chumsily written and contain reference to certain historically proved events in a most apocryphal manner. Not only they were interpolated but it appears that those who recklessly interpolated these tales had no knowledge of editing either.]

The Sun-God and His Twelve Forms

While most of the Puranas deal with Brahma, Vishnu and Shiv, the Bhavishya Purana is quite unusual as it deals with the sun god in a detailed way. It says that the sun god, Surya, manifests himself in twelve different aspects. These are called 'twelve Adityas' and their names are: Indra, Dhata, Parjanya, Pusha, Twashtha, Aryama, Bhaga, Vivaswava, Vishnu, Amshu, Varuna and Mitra. In these forms the sun god discharges his responsibilities in the following way: As

(i) **Indra**: the sun god rules all the gods and he is the divine king.

(ii) **Dhata**: the sun god creates all beings.

(iii) **Parjanya**: the sun god resides in the clouds and causes rain over the earth.

(iv) **Pusha**: the sun god exists in all food-grains and provides nourishment to all the live beings.

(v) **Twashtha**: the sun god in this form dwells in all the trees, herbs and vegetation.

(vi) **Aryama**: the sun god in this form dwells in wind and supplies live-breath to all.

(vii) **Bhaga**: the sun god in this form dwells in the earth and in the bodies of all living beings.

(viii) **Viwaswana**: the sun god in this form remains existent in the fire and aids in cooking of food.

(ix) **Vishnu**: the sun god in this form destroys the enemies of god and upholds all that is righteous.

(x) **Amshu**: the sun god in this form is present in all

that allow the growth of life and that which delights the beings.

(xi) **Varuna**: the sun god permeates water and is the sustainer of life.

(xii) **Mitra**: the sun god exists on the banks of the river Chandrabhaga. [This is the spot where Samba constructed the deity's temple.]

He who realises that this way the sun god permates every bit of universe lives as close to him as being part of himself.

In each of the twelve months one form of the sun god dwells. They are the following:

As Vishnu in the month of Chaitra, as Aryama in Vaishakha, as Vivasvana in Jyeshtha, as Amshu in Ashadha, as Parjanya in Shravan, as Varuna in Bhadra, as Indra in Ashwin, as Dhata in Kartika, as Mitra in Agrahayana, as Pousha in the month of Pausha, as Bhaga in Magha and Twashtha in Phalguna.

This way each month has a different sun god's manifestation. In fact these twelve names are nothing but names of the sun god, Surya. Apart from there the sun god is also known as: Aditya, Savita, Mihira, Arka, Prabhakara, Martanda, Bhaskara, Bhanu, Chitrabhanu, Diwakar and Ravi.

This Purana also defines the intensity of each of the twelve suns, measuring it by the number of rays:

(i)	*Vivasvana*	Fourteen hundred rays
(ii)	*Aryama*	Three hundred rays
(iii)	*Amshu*	Fifteen hundred rays
(iv)	*Parjanya*	Fourteen hundred rays
(v)	*Varuna*	Fourteen hundred rays
(vi)	*Vishnu*	Fourteen hundred rays
(vii)	*Indra*	Twelve hundred rays
(viii)	*Dhata*	Eleven hundred rays
(ix)	*Mitra*	Fifteen hundred rays
(x)	*Pousha*	One thousand rays
(xi)	*Bhaga*	Fifteen hundred rays
(xii)	*Twashtha*	One thousand rays

This is apparent that Aryama is the weakest sun. [Perhaps this is the sun which shines in the month between 15th October and 15th November, particularly in the zodiac sign Libra. Curiously enough this is not the case by this Purana as, according to the sun gods listed above, Aryama shines in Vaishaka when astrologically the sun is believed to be in Aries, its exaltation sign. This confusion has resulted due to various interpolations that the Purana is believed to have suffered.]

The Sun's Chariot: It has been vividly described. It is, by this Purana, believed to have been wrought by Brahma himself. The name of the charioteer is Aruna. (Some accounts call this charioteer to be Anuru. The chariot is drawn by seven golden horses. Their names are Gayatri, Trishtupa, Jagati, Anushtupa, Pamkti, Vrihati and Ushnika.

In this chariot two Adityas, two sages (Rishis), two Gandharvas, two Apsaras, two Nagas (serpents) and two Rakshasas always ride. Specifying as to who rides when, the Purana gives the following details: In the months of Chaitra and Vaishakha the two Adityas are Dhata and Aryama, the sages Pulastya and Pulaha, the Gandharvas Tumburu and Narada, the Apsaras Kritasthali and Punjikasthala, the Nagas Vasuki and Kachha and the Rakshasas are Heti and Prabeti.

In the months of Jyeshtha and Ashada, the Adityas are Mitra and Varuna, the sages Atri and Vashishtha, the Gandharvas Haha and Hoohoo, the Apsaras Menaka and Sahajanya, the Nagas Takshaka and Ananta (Shesh Naga) and the Rakshasas Pourusheya and Budha.

Similarly in the months of Shravana and Bhadra, the Adityas are Indra and Vivasvana, the sages Angira and Bhrigu, the Gandharvas Vishvavasu and Ugrasena, the Apsaras Pramalochana and Anulochana, the Nagas Elapatra and Shankhapala, the Rakshasas Sarpa and Vyeghra.

In the months of Ashvina and Kartika, the Adityas are Parjanya and Pousha, the sages Bharadwaja and Gautama, the Gandharvas Chitrasena and Ruchi, the Apsaras Vishvachi and Ghritachi, the Nagas Vishruta and Dhananjaya and the Rakshasas Apa and Vata.

The same way in the months of Aghrayana and Pousha, the Adityas are Amsha and Bhaga, the sages Kashyapa and Kratu, the Gandharvas Chitrangada and Urnayu, the Apsaras Purva Chitli and Urvashi, the Nagas Tarkshya and Arishtanemi and the Rakshasas Avasphurja and Vidyut.

Lastly, in the months of Magha and Phalguna, the Adityas are Twashtha and Vishnu, the sages Jamadagni and Vishwamitra, the Gandharvas Dhritarashtra and Varcha, the Apsara Tilotttama and Rambha, the Nagas Kadraveya and Kambakshvatava and the Rakshas as Brahmapreta and Yakshapreta.

The Purana ends with the assertion that those who read or listen to this Purana with rapt attention have their sins dissipated and they earn enough merit to dwell in the divine realms.

Epilogue

The last part of this Puran is called Uttar Parva which lists many stories, the most prominent one being that in which Yudhistrthir asks Lord Krishna about the being's ideal way of leading life. In fact, in this work, we have clubbed together all the relevant details in a separate chapter. The problem with this kind of ancient books is that they are generally not very well edited. Although it is believed that during the 'Golden Period of Indian History' (the Gupta Age, in the 3rd-4th centuries AD) all the Puranas were duly edited at the royal command, the later interpolations again rendered them a haphazardly joined account of the ancient period. It is for the convenience of the modern readership that we have recast its chapters by clubbing all the relevant portions under one chapter. Many of the stories or details (like the descriptors of various hells) have been deliberately omitted as their better comprehensible versions are given in other Puranas.

According the this Purana, the Srimadbhagwat Purana, in which Lord Vishnu has been glorified, is the Creation of Parashara Muni[1]. The Skanda Purana was created by Lord Shiv; the origin of the Padma Purana is believed to be the Creator, Brahma's mouth while the creation of the Brahmavaivarta Purana is attributed to Sage Shuka (Shukadeva). Lord Hari himself is believed to be the creator of the Garuda Purana. These six Puranas are said to be Sattvika Puranas.

The Puranas that are created by Sage Vedavyasa are said to be the Matsya, Koorma, Nrisimha, Varuna and Vayu Puranas. [Although the generally believed fact is that all these Puranas had been created by sage Vedavyasa, but this Purana makes this distinction. May be these Puranas

---

1. Although Parashar was the name of Sage Vedavyasa's father at several places this name is also used for the sage himself.

had their different authors but it was Sage Vedavyasa who edited all the eighteen Puranas]. Since the above mentioned Puranas are full of details of the ritual practices, they are supposed to belong to the Rajas category of the Puranas. The creation of the Varaha and Markandeya Purana is credited to Markandeya Muni. It was sage Angira who created Agni Purana, Tandi created Linga and Brahmanda Purana and for the enlightenment of the people it was Lord Shiv who created the Bhavishya Purana. These six Puranas are called Tamas Purana.

According to this Purana the best among all the Puranas is Bhagwata Purana. When Kaliyuga had become rampant over the earth, Maharaj Vikram[1] invited all the great sages dwelling over Mount Kailash (Himalayas) to Nemisharanya Teertha and he requested Soota ji to recite to them all the Puranas. At that time Soota ji also informed the king that there were 18 secondary Puranas. [Perhaps it was during that recital the vetting-editing of the Puranas must have also been undertaken. This is also the reason why all the Puranas begin with *Ekada Nemisharanye*. (or 'once in Nemisharanya'). However it is apparent that those versions of the Mahapuranas were not taken as final since the interpolations continued to be added to these Puranas rather recklessly].

In fact there are many versions of the Bhavishya Purana, not only available from different publishers but also having quite different stories and other details. The scholars opine that this Purana is believed to be a summantion of three different Puranas called (i) Bhavishya Purana, (ii) Bhavishyata purana and (iii) Bhavishyottara Purana. It is believed that the Bhavishya Purana as we have it today is a subsequent presentation of the Bhavishyata Purana. The Bhavishyottara Purana specifically deals with the keeping of fasts and giving alms, and must have originally formed a part of the Bhavishya Purana. The Bhavishyottara Purana, on its own, is an authentic and recognised work, but does not contain any of the five characterstics of Mahapurana. So when we refer the Bhavishya Purana, we, in fact, refer

---

1. Perhaps the reference is for Vikramaditya (Chandragupta II of the Gupta Dynasty), the most illustrious ruler of that dynasty.

to all the three texts. Else, the Purana would not be complete. We have tried to give reference of all the stories that are prominently mentioned in these three texts but we have deleted those which are either well known and have been given in other Puranas or which apperently seem to convey nothing of substance.

The first reference to these texts are to be found in the **Apastambha Dharma Sastra**, a work dated not later than the 3rd Century BC. But how to reconcile the allusion to the Medieval Ages or even to the British Raj in India? In order to explain this, most of the celebrated Indologists opine that this is a text that has grown over a period of 2000 years from the 3rd century BC [In the text of this work we have explained where the narration takes the present or future tenses]. The suggested upper and lower limits of the period are 450 or 500 BC to 1850 AD. In the course of this growth or evolution, later day material was added to the original stuff that formed the core material. Although the later day material was interpolated as prediction or prognostications it is apparent that the observation is coeval. Perhaps in order to maintain the sanctity of the Puranas they were incorporated as if they were foreseen by the sages of the epic period. Even the foreign influences were seen as predictions. After all, historically, India was subjected to repeated invasions and the influences of the Pahlavas, the Seythians and other Iranian-Central Asian people are very well apparent. Some of them, the Maga Brahmanas, for example, retained their identity and even showed their influence on Indian texts like this Purana.

It has been quite an effort to segregate the chaff from the grains and chapterise the text in such a way as to become most easily comprehensible even to the curious reader. The aim of this series is not to give the authentic translation to the text of the Puranas but to highlight that part which throws enough light on that formative part, even. For the people of the modern age we want this work to serve the role of the trailer to generate enough interest in the readers to go to the original.

Glossary

Aditi	Mother of Gods
Airavata	Indra's mount, a fabled elephant
Ahlaad	Dilight
Amaravati	The kingdom of the gods
Ashwins	The two (twins) of god, Ashwini Kumara
Asuras	Demons, used in the sense of negation to Sura (God)
Avataar	Incarnation
Baladeva (Balarama)	Lord Krishna's elder brother (Balabhadra)
Bhuloka	The earth, one of the three worlds.
Bhuvana	The world
Bhuvarloka	The world above the earth, below the heaven
Brahman	Divine essence of Lord Almighty
Brahmastra	The divine weapon
Chandala	A man of low caste, a pariah
Chandra Vansha	Lunar Dynasty
Dakshina	A kind of fee which must follow every Daan (alms giving)
Dhanurveda	The science of archery
Dhanavantari	The divine physician
Diti	Mother of the demons
Gayatri	The very sacred incantation, also a goddess
Govyuti	Unit of measurement
Jatismara	One who remembers the events of one's past lives
Kartikeya	God of war, Lord Shiv's eldest son
Kashtha	A small unit of time
Krishna Paksha	Dark fortnight
Loka	Region (realm)
Maruta	God of winds

Muhurta	Unit of time
Nishka	A coin (of smallest denomination)
Pativrata	Woman dedicated to her husband
Pitri	Ancestors in heaven
Prana Vayu	Vital air, breath of life
Pratisarga	Destruction of Creation
Samadhi	Deep meditation
Sandhyamsha	The period between two Yugas
Saptarshi	Great Bear Constellation
Shraddha	The annual ceremony to show gratitude to one's dead ancestors
Shukla Paksha	Bright fortnight.
Tamas	Quality associated with darkness
Tithi	Lunar day's duration
Upa-Purana	Minor Purana
Upaveeta	The sacred thread
Vanshanu Charita	History of royal dynasties
Vrata	A religious determination resolve
Yaksha	Demi-god, their lord is Kubera, the custodian of the divine wealth
Yantra	An instrument/ a machine
Yava	A small unit of time
Yojana	A unit of distance (nearly two miles)
Yuka	A unit of measurement

YOU WANT TO KNOW ABOUT...

WORLD FAMOUS WOMEN
Renu Saran

These female personalities are not just the rulers, freedom fighters and the like who are figured in the list of must read biographies in this comprehensive reference book. The list also includes famous Indian laureates and scientists, spiritual leaders and contemporary political leaders, as well as film stars & sports personalities.

Rs. 95.00

FAMOUS INDIAN WOMEN
Renu Saran

The list also includes famous Indian laureates and scientists, spiritual leaders and contemporary political leaders, as well as film stars & sports personalities.

Rs. 95.00

GREAT PERSONALITIES OF THE WORLD
Renu Saran

This book is a humble approach to compile life sketches of Great Personalities of the World in different fields, so as to act as a source of inspiration and motivation for each individual to excel in the field of activity they are related with.

Rs. 150.00

GREAT INDIAN PERSONALITIES
Renu Saran

This book is a humble approach to compile life sketches of great Indian personalities in different fields, so as to act as a source of inspiration and motivation for each individual to excel in the field of activity, they are related with.

Rs. 150.00

Diamond Pocket Books (P) Ltd.
X-30, Okhla Industrial Area, Phase-II, New Delhi-110020,
Phones : 41611861- 65, 40712100, Fax : (0091) -011- 41611766
E-mail : Sales@dpb.in, Website: www.dpb.in

⬥ DIAMOND POCKET BOOKS PRESENTS

ASTROLOGY, VAASTU, PALMISTRY & RELIGION BOOKS

Pt. V.K. Sharma
- Occult Lines on the Hands 150.00
- Shape of the Hands 95.00
- Magic Numbers 195.00

Dr. Bhojraj Dwivedi
Be your own Astrologer
- Ascendant Libra 150.00
- Ascendant Aries 150.00
- Ascendant Taurus 150.00
- Ascendant Gemini 150.00
- Ascendant Cancer 150.00
- Ascendant Leo 150.00
- Ascendant Virgo 150.00
- Ascendant Scorpio 150.00
- Ascendant Sagittarius 150.00
- Ascendant Capricorn 150.00
- Ascendant Aquarius 150.00
- Ascendant Pisces 150.00
- *Hindu Traditions and Beliefs : A Scientific Basis (Q & A) 150.00
- *Hindu Traditions and Beliefs (A Religious Validity) 95.00
- *Feng Shui : Chinese Vaastu Shastra 195.00
- *Pyramid and Temple Vaastu 195.00
- *Yantra, Mantra, Tantra and Occult Science 195.00
- *Thumb! The Mirror of Fate 150.00
- *Astrology & Wealth (Jyotish Aur Dhyan Yog) 95.00
- *Jyotish Aur Rajyog 95.00
- *Jyotish and Santan Yog 75.00
- *Remedial Vaastushastra 200.00
- *Sampuran Vaastushastra 200.00
- *Commercial Vaastushastra 200.00
- *Environmental Vaastu 150.00
- *The Mystique of Gems & Stones (4 colour) 250.00
- *Kalsarp Yoga Aur Ghatvivah (in Press) 200.00
- *The Mystical of Palmistry 295.00
- *Study of Omens 95.00
- *The Astrological Analysis of Earthquake 60.00

S.N. Mathur, B. K. Chaturvedi
- Hindu Gods and Goddesses 295.00

Er. R. Prasad
- Magic of Feng Shui 120.00
- Magic of Vaastu Shashtra 120.00

Shashi Kant Oak
- *Naadi Prediction 95.00

Manish Verma
- *Fast & Festivals of India 95.00

Pt. Gopal Sharma, Dr. D.P. Rao
- *Pyramid Power & Vaastu 195.00
- *Advance Feng Shui (For Health and Happiness) 195.00
- *Sri Sai Science of Griha Vaastu 195.00
- *Vaastu and Pyramidal Remidies 195.00

Pt. Gopal Sharma
- *Comprehensive Vaastu 75.00
- *Wonders of Numbers 95.00

Acharya Vipul Rao
- *Hypnotism 95.00

Cheiro
- *Cheiro's Language of the Hand (Palmistry) 95.00
- *Cheiro's Book of Numerology 60.00
- *Cheiro's Astro Numerology & Your Star 95.00
- *Cheiro's Book of Astrology 95.00

B.R. Chuwdhary
- *Speed Palmistry with Memory Tips 95.00

A. Somasundaram
- *Future is in Our Hands 90.00

S. K. Sharma
- *The Brilliance of Hinduism 95.00
- *Sanskar Vidhi (Arya Samaj) 95.00

Dr. B.R. Kishore
- *Hinduism 95.00
- *Essence of Vedas 195.00
- *Mahabharata 75.00
- *Ramayana 75.00
- *Supreme Mother Goddesses Durga (4 Colour Durga Chalisa) 95.00

Dr. Raj Bali Pandey
- *Rigveda 95.00
- *Samveda 95.00
- *Yajurveda 95.00
- *Atharvveda 95.00

Manan Sharma
- *Buddhism (Teachings of Buddha) 95.00
- *Universality of Buddha 95.00

Anurag Sharma
- *Life Profile & Biography of Buddha 95.00
- *Thus Spake Buddha 95.00

Udit Sharma
- *Teaching & Philosophy of Buddha 95.00

Pt. Radha Krishna Shrimali
- Lal Kitab 150.00

Order books by V.P.P. Postage Rs. 20/- per book extra. Postage free on order of three or more books. Send Rs. 20/- in advance.

⬥ DIAMOND POCKET BOOKS (P) LTD.
X-30, Okhla Industrial Area, Phase-II, New Delhi-110020.
Phones : 41611861, Fax : (0091) -011- 41611866.
E-mail : sales@diamondpublication.com, Website : www.dpb.in

Diamond Books Presents

Dynamic Memory Common Errors in English
Tarun Chakarbory

English is a widely used language in our business & professional environment and further in corporate world it is a must. It may be very closely observed that for most of the times, the English used by people is not correct, yet it is spoken and written out of ignorence in the same way. Such show is rated as very bad by learned people. This book by Tarun Chakarborty is a result of his great efforts where he has identified such common errors and presented their correct use. **Rs. 110.00**

Dynamic Memory Perfect Spoken in English
Tarun Chakarbory

English speaking is generally latest as a impressive tool among all class of people. But for most of the times the spoken English is not correct rather it is full of errors. At a glance, such incorrect spoken English is marked behind fluency but it is categorised as a poor show by learned people. This valuable book of Tarun Chakarborty is a meaning full effort to catch the attention of people to correct themselves. The book provides a lot of material to meet the objective. **Rs. 110.00**

Dynamic Memory Idioms & Phrases
Tarun Chakarbory

This book 'Dynamic Memory Idioms & Phrases' is well written by Sri Tarun Chakarborty to offer a huge collection of idioms, with this idiomatic origin and further their meaning. The idioms are arranged in alphabatic order which is of great help to book user 'the help is further supplemented by content index given at the begin of the book. The book is certainly very valuable for student & English lovers. **Rs. 95.00**

Dynamic Memory Group Discussions
Tarun Chakarbory

Group discussion is a very effective tool to select propes manpower for any good jobs. A candidate has to project his skills of expression to the board, at the same times has to slow that he is good to work in a team, while he is a brilliant leader like person as well. It is a tought experience to overcome group discussion if one is not practical & orient for such game. This book by Tarun Chakarborty steps to predseup this gap and tends to remove the obvious hitch in the candidates. **Rs. : 95.00**

Dynamic Memory Sure Success in Interview
Tarun Chakarbory

When you are invited to an interview it means that the hiring manager believes you may be a good match for the job opening, she or he want to know for sure. This book is a ready reckoner for those who want to present themselves in a powerful & prossive way. **Rs. : 95.00**

Dynamic Memory Synoniums & Antonimous Dictionary
Tarun Chakarbory

Communication is effective when we have a firm grip on vocabulary. Anyone should make the reader's job easier by communicating whatever he or she wants to communicate.
Not only does reading allow you to build up your vocabulary, but it also allows you to become more informed, learning things about the world around you. **Rs. : 95.00**

Books can be requisitioned by V.P.P. Postage charges will be Rs. 20/- per book.
For orders of three books the postage will be free.

 **DIAMOND BOOKS** X-30, Okhla Industrial Area, Phase-II, New Delhi-110020,
Phone : 41611861 Fax : 41611866
E-mail : sales@dpb.in Website : www.dpb.in

DIAMOND POCKET BOOKS PRESENTS
SHIRDI SAI & RELIGIOUS BOOKS

B. Umamashwara Rao
The Spiritual Philosophy of
Shri Shirdi Sai Baba 150.00
Communications from the
Spirit of Shirdi Sai Baba 80.00
Sri Shirdi Sai Baba 60.00
Thus Spake Sri Shirdi Sai Baba 40.00

Dr. S.P. Ruhela (Com. & Ed.)
Sri Shirdi Sai Baba : The Unique
Prophet of Integration 150.00
The Immortal Fakir of Shirdi 150.00
Sai Grace and Recent Predictions 95.00
The Divine Glory of Shri Shirdi Sai Baba 60.00
[Experience of Devotees in the
Post-Samadhi Period (1918-1997)]
Shirdi Sai : The Supreme 80.00
Divine Grace of Sri Shirdi Sai Baba 150.00
Divine Revealations of a Sai Devotee 95.00
Sri Shirdi Sai Bhjanavali (In Roman) 50.00
Worship of Sri Sathya Sai Baba (In Roman) . 40.00
World Peace and Sri Sathya Sai Avtar 60.00
How to Receive Sri Sathya Sai Baba's Grace .. 100.00
Sri Sathya Sai Baba : Understanding
His Mystery and Experiencing His Love 95.00

Chakor Ajgaonkar
The Footprints of Shirdi Sai 100.00
Tales from Sai Baba's Life 75.00

B.K. Chaturvedi
Sai Baba of Shirdi 60.00
The Miracle Man : Sri Sathya Sai Baba 75.00

S. Maaney
The Eternal Sai 40.00

Sushila Devi Ruhela
Sri Shirdi Sai Bhajanmala (Roman) 10.00

Yogi M. K. Spencer
Rare Mesage's from
Shri Shirdi Sai Baba as God 60.00
Shri Sainath Mananam 50.00

RELIGIOUS BOOKS

Pt. Ramesh Tiwari
Shrimad Bhagvad Gita Krishna
The Charioteer 150.00

Vinay Surya
Mokshya Dwar 150.00

Narendra Kohli
Initiation (Ram Katha) 150.00

Dhananjaya Kumar
Soul Speaks to the Seeker 195.00

Swami Chinmayanand
The Holy Geeta 300.00

Dr. Giriraj Sharan Agarwal
Mahatma Kabir & His Poetry 95.00
Guru Nanak & His Poetry 95.00
Meera Bai & His Poetry 95.00

Roman Books for NRI's
Kaliupasana (including Chandi Path) 95.00
Durga Saptashati 60.00
Bhajan, Lokgeet or Aartiyan
(Roman English, Hindi) 95.00
Hindu Vrat Kathayen (Including
Saptvaar Vrat Kathayen) 50.00
Chalisa Sangreh (Including Aarties in Roman) .. 60.00
Shri Satya Narayana Vrat Katha
(English and Hindi) 25.00
Sanatan Dharm Pooja 95.00
Sudha kalp 95.00
Shiv Abhisek Poojan 25.00
Daily Prayer (Hindi, English, French, Roman) . 25.00
Sanatan Daily Prayer 25.00
Durga Chalisa 10.00
Gaytari Chalisa 10.00
Shiv Chalisa 10.00
Hanuman Chalisa 10.00
Shri Sai Chalisa 10.00
Selected Song of Rafi 60.00
Selected Song of Lata 60.00
Selected Song of Kishore 60.00
Selected Song of Mukesh 60.00
Filmi & Non-filmi Songs 195.00
......
The Hymns & Orisons of Lord Shiva (Roman) 30.00
Sri Hanuman Chalisa (Roman) 30.00
Pilgrimage Centres of India 95.00
Chalisa Sangreh 60.00

Himalayan Institute of Yoga
Pandit Rajmani Tigunait, Ph.D.
Seven Systems of Indian Philosophy 200.00
Touched by Fire 295.00
The Power of Mantra &
the Mystery of Initiation 175.00
Why We Fight 150.00

Swami Veda Bharati
God 200.00
Meditation and the Art of Dying 200.00

Swami Rama
Life Here and Hereafter 150.00
Choosing A Path 250.00
A Practical Guide to Holistic Health 200.00

DIAMOND BOOKS X-30, Okhla Industrial Area, Phase-II, New Delhi-110020,
Phone : 011-40712100, Fax : 011-41611866, E-mail : sales@dpb.in, Website : www.dpb.in